Reading the
APOSTOLIC
FATHERS

Reading the

APOSTOLIC

FATHERS

An Introduction

CLAYTON N. JEFFORD

with KENNETH J. HARDER *and*
LOUIS D. AMEZAGA, JR.

HENDRICKSON
PUBLISHERS

ISBN 1–56563–154–4

First Printing — October 1996

Library of Congress Cataloging-in-Publication Data

Jefford, Clayton N.
    Reading the Apostolic Fathers   /   Clayton N. Jefford, with
Kenneth J. Harder and Louis D. Amezaga, Jr.
    Includes bibliographical references and index.
    ISBN 1–56563–154–4
    1. Apostolic Fathers.   I. Harder, Kenneth J.   II. Amezaga,
Louis D.   III. Title
BR60.A65J44   1996
270.1—dc20   96–10730
                                                            CIP

In memory of
Sr. John Bosco Sanders, C.PP.S.
of the Sisters of the Most Precious Blood
O'Fallon, Missouri
(4 April 1923–31 August 1994)

Table of Contents

List of Figures and Maps

Acknowledgments

It is appropriate that we express our appreciation to several persons who have helped to make this volume possible. A word of thanks is due to the many students of the Saint Meinrad Seminary who agreed to read through sections of the manuscript in order to ensure that the materials were both clear and useful. Their suggestions have often proven to be enlightening. Among these students, Mr. David Reinhart has been especially helpful in the production of maps for the volume. We are particularly grateful to Professor Richard C. Stern, assistant professor of homiletics at the Saint Meinrad School of Theology, who took precious time from his sabbatical schedule in the spring of 1995 to read a final draft of the manuscript and to offer numerous valuable corrections to the text. Also, our appreciation is extended to Mr. Patrick H. Alexander, at Hendrickson Publishers, both for his interest in this project and for his patience.

For the Reader

It is our hope that this little book will serve as a quick and simple introduction to a unique collection of early Christian writings, the so-called apostolic fathers. These materials are intended to function only as a guide or an introduction. The reader certainly will need to read the writings themselves. A list of English translations is provided below.

Other more extensive surveys of the apostolic fathers are available, of course, but these tend to be expensive, hard to obtain, or difficult to use except by specialists in early church history. In addition, nearly all such surveys in English currently are out of print. Our book attempts to avoid some of the typical problems of introductions. It has been written with the assistance of students and is designed for those who read and work at either the college, seminary, or graduate level. The book does not assume that the reader has any particular knowledge of early church history or any broad background in biblical studies or early Christian literature. The goal of our introduction is to be clear and concise, easy to read, intelligible, and suitable for reading in short periods of time as the student's schedule permits.

The format of the book is designed to be convenient either for the classroom setting or for individual study. A general statement about the history and literature of the apostolic fathers is provided at the beginning, followed by nine chapters featuring the individual writings that commonly are included among the apostolic fathers. In an attempt to assist the student, we have divided each chapter into four main sections:

—ANSWERS *(a brief summary of information about the relevant text)*

—QUESTIONS *(an exploration of those details that make each text unique)*

—CONTENTS *(an outline and summary of what can be found in the text)*

—RELATED LITERATURE *(a brief list of relevant studies in English)*

We realize that a student can best come to understand history and its literature only to the extent that she or he reflects upon the QUESTIONS of any particular writing, that is, those details that make a given text unique (considered in the second part of each chapter). Yet there is something of a practical nature to a book that allows the student to *begin* with an ANSWERS section—a concise, easy-to-find summary of data about each text for those times such as before a quiz, in the heat of a group discussion, or in the last-minute preparation of a paper.

In addition to the four-part division of each chapter, this book is simplified in a second way. The information in each chapter is arranged according to an outline format so that individual issues can be defined and discussed without confusion. As an aid for the reader, each item in the ANSWERS section is numbered to reflect the location of the corresponding discussion in the QUESTIONS section. For example, if a student wanted to find out who we think wrote the Letter of Barnabas, he or she would look under the heading "1.1.3" (which indicates *chapter* 1 = Letter of Barnabas; *section* 1 = AN-SWERS; *item* 3 = Authorship). In order to discover how we came to our conclusions, the student would then look under the corresponding heading of "1.2.3" (which indicates *chapter* 1 = Letter of Barnabas; *section* 2 = QUESTIONS; *item* 3 = Who was the author?). It is our hope that this reference system will help each reader in finding specific information as quickly as possible.

Important, new, or difficult words and phrases appear in **boldface.** These are gathered into a glossary at the end of the book. Charts, lists, and maps are located throughout the book as an aid to learning about the texts. There are no footnotes or endnotes for the student to ignore or skip. Abbreviations of technical terms are avoided in order to keep the text clear and obvious. Finally, books listed in the RELATED LITERATURE sections are provided with their Library of Congress numbers in order to encourage the reader to utilize additional resources in the further study of the apostolic fathers. The reader should be aware, of course, that some libraries list their copies of these books according to another system of classification, or they alter the Library of Congress system to meet their own institutional needs.

ENGLISH TRANSLATIONS OF THE APOSTOLIC FATHERS

Burton, Edward. *The Apostolic Fathers.* 2 vols. Edinburgh: John Grant, 1909. Out of print. (BQ1080.A4 1909)

Glimm, Francis X., Joseph M.-F. Marique, and Gerald G. Walsh. *The Apostolic Fathers: A New Translation.* Fathers of the Church 1. Edited by L. Schopp. New York: Cima, 1947. Out of print. (BQ1080.A4 1947)

Goodspeed, Edgar J. *The Apostolic Fathers: An American Translation.* New York: Harper and Brothers, 1950. Out of print. (GH1.5.G655 1950)

Grant, Robert M., ed. *The Apostolic Fathers: A New Translation and Commentary.* 6 vols. New York and Camden, N.J.: Thomas Nelson & Sons, 1964–68. Out of print. (BQ1080.A4 1964)

Lake, Kirsopp. *The Apostolic Fathers.* 2 vols. Loeb Classical Library 24/25. Cambridge, Mass.: Harvard University Press, 1977; London: William Heinemann, 1977. Original translation is 1912–13. (PA3611.A7 1977)

Lightfoot, J. B., and J. R. Harmer. *The Apostolic Fathers.* Revised and edited by M. W. Holmes. 2d ed. Grand Rapids, Mich.: Baker Book House, 1992. Original translation is 1891. (BR60.A62 1992)

Quasten, Johannes, and Joseph C. Plumpe, eds. *Ancient Christian Writers* 1/6. Translated by J. A. Kleist. Westminster, Md.: Newman, 1946–48. Does not include 2 Clement or the Shepherd of Hermas. (BQ314.A5 1946)

Richardson, Cyril C., E. R. Fairweather, E. R. Hardy, and M. H. Shepherd. *Early Christian Fathers.* Library of Christian Classics 1. New York: Macmillan, 1970. Original translation is 1953. Does not include Barnabas or the Shepherd of Hermas. (BQ5216.L5 1970)

Roberts, Alexander, and James Donaldson, eds. *Ante-Nicene Fathers.* Revised by A. C. Coxe. Peabody, Mass.: Hendrickson, 1989. Original translation is 1866–72. (BQ334.A4 1989)

Sparks, Jack, ed. *The Apostolic Fathers.* Nashville and New York: Thomas Nelson, 1978. Out of print. Does not include the Letter to Diognetus. (BR60.A62 1978)

Staniforth, Maxwell. *Early Christian Writings: The Apostolic Fathers.* Revised by A. Louth. The Penguin Classics L197. New York: Penguin Books, 1987. Original translation is 1968. Does not include 2 Clement or the Shepherd of Hermas. (BR60.A62.E2 1968)

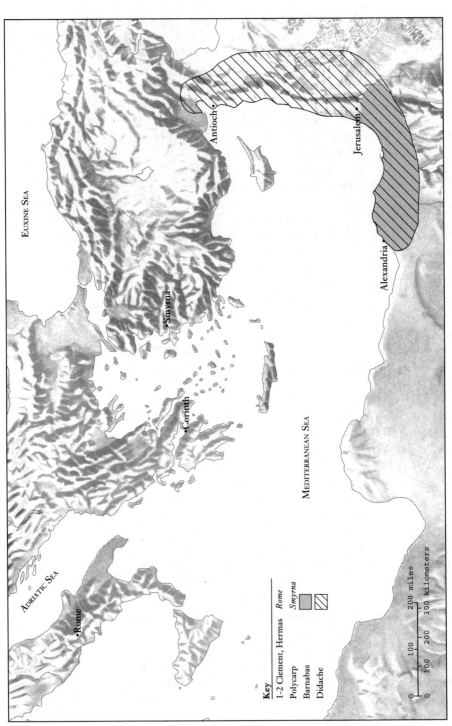

THE APOSTOLIC FATHERS IN THE MEDITERRANEAN WORLD

Key
1-2 Clement, Hermas   *Rome*
Polycarp   *Smyrna*
Barnabas
Didache

200 miles
300 kilometers

Introduction:
What Are the Apostolic Fathers?

Historians have assigned the phrase "apostolic fathers" to a narrow collection of early Christian texts dating from the first and second centuries AD. These texts, which were written by leaders of the early church over the course of nearly one hundred years, originally did not circulate as a single collection. Instead, they were assembled into one form or another over the centuries; ultimately they became a vaguely unified selection of materials. The title "apostolic fathers" itself was not applied to these materials in antiquity but is instead a modern designation that distinguishes the writings from other collections of early Christian literature, such as the New Testament and the so-called New Testament **Apocrypha.**

Most church historians think that the phrase "apostolic fathers" was first applied to the texts during the late seventeenth century. In 1672 the French scholar J. B. Cotelier, a specialist in the field of **patristics,** used the Latin phrase *patres aevi apostolici* (or in English translation, "Fathers of the Apostolic Period") as part of the title for his two-volume work on these early Christian writings. Cotelier reflected the common view of the times that each writing in the collection had come from an early Christian author who knew one or more of the first-century apostles (the first followers of Jesus of Nazareth), or who at least had received instruction from the disciples of the apostles. As a result, the teachings and sources contained in these writings were believed to reflect some of the earliest testimonies of faith in the ancient church—the testimonies of the original apostles of Christianity.

There is little question that the collection includes several texts that are as old as the writings of the New Testament itself. Early Christian writers, much like the New Testament authors, generally recognized the Hebrew Scriptures—which Christians know today as the Old Testament—as their source of literary authority. At the same time certain passages in the apostolic fathers have parallels in New Testament literature; but in a way these did not reflect any particular awareness of the usage and setting of those parallels. Finally, numerous early church theologians and historians considered some of these texts themselves to carry the authority of scripture, though ultimately none of them were included in the final form of the Christian biblical **canon** of today.

As is the case with the New Testament, the number of texts in the Fathers has become defined through a slow process. In his own edition, Cotelier included the Letter of Barnabas, the letters of Ignatius, the Letter of Polycarp, the Martyrdom of Polycarp, 1–2 Clement, and the Shepherd of Hermas. A century later in 1765, A. Gallandi added the Letter to Diognetus to this collection, together with the apology of Quadratus and the fragments of Papias. Since its discovery in the late nineteenth century, the Didache also has been included among this list of texts. Recent editions of the apostolic fathers usually include most of these writings, while the materials of Quadratus and Papias typically are omitted (for this reason, no introduction to either of these texts is included here).

Most of these writings were virtually unknown until the sixteenth century. The few manuscripts containing the various writings that now form the Fathers are preserved primarily in the libraries of monasteries scattered throughout Europe. These texts presumably were safe from the general lack of respect for ancient literature which characterized the Middle Ages. Unfortunately for modern scholars, however, some of the manuscripts were edited and reshaped by copyists of devout faith who wanted the writings to represent either their own theological perspectives or the doctrinal positions of the institutional church. Perhaps the best illustration of this process is found in the letters of Ignatius, which became expanded and corrupted by scribes over the years. Other texts remained outside of general circulation for centuries and for all practical purposes were lost. It was only through accident, for example, that the text of the Didache was *rediscovered* in 1883.

The Nature of the Collection

The apostolic fathers include a variety of different literary forms. The most common form is the letter or epistle. Included here are the seven genuine letters of Ignatius (which some traditions have combined with six letters from a later, unknown author), a letter from Rome which has become associated with the early bishop Clement (= 1 Clement), and a letter by the bishop Polycarp. Three other texts are preserved in the form of a letter, though scholars question whether these writings were ever really actual letters: (a) 2 Clement, which probably is an ancient homily or short sermon that has been attributed by tradition to Clement of Rome; (b) the Letter of Barnabas, which is a sermon or theological tract by an unknown author; and (c) the Letter to Diognetus, an early **apology,** or defense of the Christian faith, that appears to have combined a short, ancient letter and a fragment of an early homily.

In addition to the letter form, the works of the apostolic fathers exhibit other literary genres that circulated widely in the early church. The Shepherd of Hermas, for instance, consists of several early Christian sources that combine to form an example of what is known as **apocalyptic literature,** or writings considered to be the direct revelation of eternal truths by divine figures. A widely recognized example of this literary style outside of the apostolic fathers is the book of Revelation in the New Testament. The Didache represents yet a third category—an early manual of Christian teaching designed to instruct new converts to the faith and to direct community leaders in their work. Such manuals were popular in the early church, and many depended on the Didache for their form and teachings.

The dates for the apostolic fathers are not certain in many cases, yet it seems that the final form of each text falls sometime between AD 90 and the last third of the second century. Of course, a text's final form says nothing about the date of the sources behind it. Sources may come from as early as AD 50, when the apostles Paul and Peter preached throughout the Mediterranean world. The collection is special in that it contains information about the early expansion of Christianity not found in the New Testament. The Letter of Barnabas, for example, gives us a clue about the views of early Christian authors in Egypt, a region where Christianity quickly grew into a strong religious presence, but about which little today is known. The Didache is a list of instructions for use in the early second-century church. It reveals a specific early community's attempts to establish some understanding of how the institutional church should conduct its activities. The letters of Ignatius, together with the Letter of Polycarp, tell us much about the development of early Christian doctrines in Asia Minor (modern Turkey) after the time of Paul's work

The Dates of Composition

in that same region. The letter of 1 Clement reveals the continuing struggle of Christianity at Corinth in ancient Greece from the perspective of the church at Rome, once again after the time of Peter and Paul. Together with the Shepherd of Hermas, 1 Clement (and perhaps 2 Clement) affords additional insight into the situation in Rome at the beginning of the second century. The Letter to Diognetus, which is without question the most recent writing in the collection, was written as a defense for the Christian faith as Christianity began to spread throughout the Mediterranean world.

Figure A — WHEN WERE THE TEXTS OF THE APOSTOLIC FATHERS WRITTEN?

	AD 50	100	150	200
Letter of Barnabas				
Didache				
Letters of Ignatius				
Letter of Polycarp		13 1, 12, 14		
Martyrdom of Polycarp				
1 Clement				
2 Clement				
Shepherd of Hermas		1–24 25–114		
Letter to Diognetus				

///////// Possible   □ Probable

The Apostolic Fathers and Early Christianity

As a collection, the literature of the apostolic fathers includes texts originating throughout the Roman Empire. It is only natural, therefore, that many different forms of early Christian thought, worship, and church organization are represented in this small group of writings. This variety of perspectives and insights certainly enhances their value as a resource for study. Beyond this witness to the thoughts of the early church, many of the texts preserve early sources and traditions that otherwise would have been lost. Included here, for example, are ancient hymns and creeds. The texts also reflect the thoughts and beliefs of Christian thinkers whose views often were rejected by later theologians. The modern reader can find traditions here that were used in early worship services and that served as the guides for how Christian communities conducted their daily affairs.

Many scholars place a significant value on the Fathers because of the bridge these writings form between the texts of the New

Testament and those of later Christian authors. In many respects the Fathers parallel the literary forms and theological interests of New Testament documents. On the one hand, they address the immediate problems in specific Christian communities. At the same time, they reveal a pastoral sensitivity when their authors are forced to confront the broad issues of God's revelation to humanity as it intersected with the rise of the religious traditions of human faith. In many respects, therefore, the apostolic fathers preserve an additional piece of history about the course of early Christianity following the death of the first apostles.

The apostolic fathers are significant for yet another reason. Before the broader church agreed on a single, authoritative collection of writings—or **canon**—that ultimately became the scriptures of Christianity, many of the writings in the apostolic fathers were considered to have the authority of scripture. Thus the modern reader often finds that portions of the apostolic fathers have been quoted as scripture among the later theologians of the church. By the time of **Athanasius**, the bishop of Alexandria who listed those texts he considered authoritative for the church in AD 367, the apostolic fathers had been excluded from the New Testament **canon**.

Figure B — Who Read the Apostolic Fathers?

	Barn	Did	Ignat	Poly	Mart Pol	1 Clem	2 Clem	Shep	Diog
Irenaeus (ca. 130–200)	?		√	√		√		√	
Clement of Alexandria (ca. 150–215)	√	√	?			√		√	√
Tertullian (ca. 160–225)	√			√	√	√		√	
Hippolytus (ca. 170–236)								?	
Origen (ca. 185–254)	√		√		√	√		√	
Eusebius of Caesarea (ca. 260–340)	√	√	√	√	√	√		√	?
Athanasius (ca. 296–373)		√	√					√	
Jerome (ca. 342–420)	√		√			√		√	

The apostolic fathers hardly could be called a rich source of theological speculation or religious philosophy, such as the writings of Augustine, Martin Luther, or Karl Barth. Instead, the apostolic fathers are more concerned with practical problems that emerged with the development of individual church communities in the first and second centuries. How should churches conduct their worship services? What should new converts be taught about Christian ethics and their duty within the fledgling community? Who has the authority to speak for the resurrected Christ in each community? Who makes the final decision when disputes arise between communities? Should Christians preserve the teachings and customs of Judaism, or should such traditions be avoided? What should a community do about Christians who have strayed from the gospel faith, but who now wish to return to the fold? Which images from the Old Testament are most acceptable as prophecy for the new Christian faith? What does it mean to be a Christian?

Most of these questions have been answered in some form for contemporary Christians by the guidelines of modern church denominations and the convictions of individual faith traditions. The roots for the establishment of these guidelines and traditions often may be found in the apostolic fathers. They themselves exemplify how this very process was initiated within the church. Unfortunately, many of the same concerns and issues that were raised by these texts and that plagued early communities persist among Christians today!

The authors of the literature of the apostolic fathers have been enshrined within the memory of the Christian tradition. Here are the thoughts and concerns of the prestigious leaders of the ancient church—from the Christian leadership of Rome's empire in the West, such as Clement (bishop of Rome), to the Christian authorities of Rome's empire in the East, such as Ignatius (bishop of Antioch) and Polycarp (bishop of Smyrna). In the writings of these figures from history the modern student can discover the concerns for theology and salvation which challenged the rise of early Christians and their views of life. These people lived in a time of religious transition. They stood at the forefront of a new age of faith. It was in the hands of such persons that the hammers and chisels of religious speculation shaped Christianity's earliest confessions of belief. The writings of the Fathers preserve the results of their labors for later generations. These writings offer specific comments on issues that have come to form the basis of modern theology and ethics.

The Theologies of the Apostolic Fathers

The theologies of the apostolic fathers reflect the common mentality of the Roman Empire at its height, yet preserve the divergencies of individual communities in their quest to determine what it meant to be a Christian in the early days of the church. While the perspectives of the apostolic fathers are not unified, they do tend to share various assumptions, some of which may be readily identified:

The future of the church. The first Christians were convinced that Jesus of Nazareth—the man whom Christian faith proclaimed had been crucified, resurrected, and had ascended into heaven—would return to earth in their lifetime to establish the heavenly reign of God. This conviction, though evident throughout the several perspectives in the New Testament, is most clearly expressed in the letters of Paul. Historians find some support for a similar belief in the Letter of Barnabas, the Didache, Ignatius, and the Shepherd of Hermas. At the same time, however, the general mood of the apostolic fathers reveals a basic shift in the early Christian assumption concerning the return of Christ (also known as the *parousia*). For the most part, the early second-century church had come to accept that any such return had been delayed. Consequently, it became imperative for church leaders to determine how Christians could regulate their daily affairs within a community of believers. Foundational concerns in this regard soon arose. Who would direct the church and how would its members relate to one another? What traditions accurately represented the teachings of Jesus and the directives of the apostles? What were the appropriate forms of worship and liturgy in the Christian assembly? Who could be included within the early Christian communities, and what was to be done when problems arose? The apostolic fathers address questions such as these; this makes them an indispensable resource for understanding the development of the institutional church.

Creator—Christ—Holy Spirit. There does not appear to be any unified perspective among early Christian thinkers with respect to the nature of God. While the New Testament Gospels, especially the Gospels of Matthew and Luke, reveal a murky understanding that God can be variously understood, the primary understanding of God in the early church was oriented toward the Jewish confession of monotheism—*there is but one God!* This view was only natural, of course, since the earliest Christians were in fact Christian Jews whose faith developed as they continued their lives within the framework of Judaism, its culture, and its institutions. The inclusion of non-Jews, or Gentiles, however, introduced new ways of understanding God. The writings of the apostolic fathers reflect a time in which the early church embraced a variety of ways of understanding God, before the issue was broadly defined by later church councils.

For example, on the one hand, the Didache offers no clear distinction between a faith in God and a faith in Christ, as is evident from the frequent use of the term *Lord,* which can be interpreted as the reader might choose. The author of 2 Clement, on the other hand, admits a formal association between God and Christ, yet shows no particular concern for the place of the Spirit. At the same time, the Shepherd of Hermas is specifically concerned for the function of the Spirit within the Christian community. As part of the imagery used to depict this role of the Spirit, the author gives a more concrete vision of Christ as the master who directs the construction of the church. Thus the modern reader can see that the apostolic fathers reflect the gradual development of early Christian speculation about the nature of God. Eventually this speculation came to form the doctrinal confession of the church that God is one being with three distinctions—Creator, Christ, and Holy Spirit. Though no single text of the apostolic fathers makes such an explicit confession, each reveals the struggles of its author to formulate a uniquely Christian understanding of God.

How to live as a Christian. Perhaps one of the most distinct and pervasive concerns in the apostolic fathers is for the appropriate Christian lifestyle. Those texts that appear to preserve portions of early Christian homilies—Letter of Barnabas, 2 Clement, Shepherd of Hermas, Letter to Diognetus—directly charge specific communities to live by a certain ethical teaching. In many cases this teaching tends to be primarily Jewish and depends largely upon Old Testament standards, as in the case of Barnabas 18–20 and Didache 1–5. In other instances, there is a clear influence from Greek philosophy (though not from pagan religion) and a more general understanding of what it means to live appropriately, as is apparent in the Shepherd of Hermas and the Letter to Diognetus. Extensive evidence throughout this literature attests that the church was concerned to establish itself as a responsible religious expression within the Mediterranean world. This effort was undertaken in the face of persecutions by Roman emperors—**Nero, Domitian, Trajan**—and in the light of the realization that the Roman Empire officially recognized only two forms of religion: worship of the emperor and Judaism. For early Christians to assume a lifestyle which was distinct from common practices, therefore, was to invite disaster. It was only natural that eventually a text like the Shepherd of Hermas was needed to address the problem of Christians who, though they had once denied the church in the face of persecution, wished to return to an active life of faith within the walls of the Christian community.

The struggle for self-definition. From its beginnings Christianity identified closely with its mother religion, Judaism. Over the years, however, non-Jews were attracted to the Christian faith and their presence strained the traditional structure of the Jewish synagogue. Born out of this strain and without a clear sense of self-identity, the church was forced out of the synagogue into a hostile world of competing religious perspectives. Some writers, including the bishop Ignatius and the authors of the Letter of Barnabas and the Martyrdom of Polycarp, were quite concerned to distinguish Christianity from Judaism. The ideas and actions of the Jews are attacked in these texts in an attempt to justify the claims of Christianity as a new and pure worship of God. Yet a second threat to Christian attempts at self-identity came from non-Jewish religions. Ignatius, for example, speaks boldly against the teachings of the **mystery religions** and **docetism** which characterized much Greek thought of the time. Idol worship is similarly denounced in the Letter to Diognetus, and pagan lifestyles are rejected by the Didache. While the apostolic fathers represent a period of uncertainty in which the early church attempted to define itself as a valid religious faith, the struggle to legitimate Christianity continued among Christian theologians and historians until the early fourth century when the faith gained official and legal status under **Constantine the Great.**

There is no specific starting point in a quest to understand the apostolic fathers. In some respects it would be best to start with the oldest writings of the collection and then proceed to those reflecting a more recent historical situation. Unfortunately, however, it is not always easy to assign a date to many of the texts. At the same time, the concerns and issues in each of the texts are distinctly associated with the community for which they were produced. There is no clear, traceable course of theological development or institutional awareness from one author to the next. For these reasons, we have decided to introduce the writings in a geographical sequence—beginning with Egypt (at the southeastern corner of the Roman Empire), moving around the coast of Palestine to Asia Minor (at the northeastern corner of the empire), and concluding with the city of Rome (the political hub of the empire). This approach is fortunate in that it introduces the reader to most of the older texts first, though it should be noted that there are some exceptions to this general rule. In any case, a certain breadth of understanding can be gained by

viewing the rise of early Christianity from the distant regions of the Roman Empire before attempting to assess the church at Rome, which ultimately became the center of Christianity in medieval Europe.

R E L A T E D   L I T E R A T U R E

Altaner, Berthold. *Patrology.* Translated by H. C. Graef. Freiburg: Herder and Herder, 1960. (BQ144.A53 1960)

Cross, F. L. *The Early Christian Fathers.* London: Gerald Duckworth, 1960. (BQ147.C7 1960)

Ferguson, Everett, ed. *Encyclopedia of Early Christianity.* New York and London: Garland Publishing, 1990. (BR162.2.E53 1990)

Freedman, David Noel, ed. *The Anchor Bible Dictionary.* 6 vols. New York: Doubleday, 1992. (BS440.A54 1992)

Grant, Robert M. *The Apostolic Fathers: An Introduction.* The Apostolic Fathers 1. New York: Thomas Nelson & Sons, 1964. (BQ1080.A4 1964)

Larson, John. *A Theological and Historical Introduction to the Apostolic Fathers.* New York: Macmillan, 1961. (BQ1080.L3 1961)

Lightfoot, J. B. *The Apostolic Fathers.* 3 vols. 2d ed. London: Macmillan, 1989–90; Peabody, Mass.: Hendrickson, 1989. (BQ1080.A2 1981)

Quasten, Johannes. *Patrology.* Vol. 1, *The Beginnings of Patristic Literature.* Utrecht: Spectrum, 1950; Westminster, Md.: Christian Classics, 1990. (BQ144.Q3 1990)

Robinson, Thomas A. *The Early Church: An Annotated Bibliography of Literature in English.* The American Theological Library Association Bibliographies Series 33. London and Metuchen, N.J.: A.T.L.A. and Scarecrow, 1993. (BR162.2.R63 1993)

Tugwell, Simon. *The Apostolic Fathers.* Harrisburg, Pa.: Morehouse, 1990. (BR67.T84 1990)

1   The Letter of Barnabas

1.1.1   Manuscript tradition—two Greek texts (complete); nine short Greek texts (chapters 5–21) combined with Polycarp; one Latin text (chapters 1–17); quotations in Clement of Alexandria; brief Syriac fragments; reflections in *Apostolic Church Order*; parallel in Didache 1–6

1.1.2   Literary form—letter constructed from a homily (or treatise) and a code of conduct

1.1.3   Authorship—unknown non-Jewish Christian (name of Barnabas applied for authority)

1.1.4   Date—AD 70–135 (probably around AD 96–100)

1.1.5   Setting—Egypt (probably Alexandria)

1.1.6   Purpose—to support Christian faith with the knowledge of God's three doctrines

1.1.7   Primary elements—redefinition of Judaism; concern for end times; special knowledge

1.1.8   Special images—scapegoat; red heifer; Jesus revealed in the number 318

1.1.9   Relationship to scripture—primary focus upon thematic collections of Old Testament texts; specific focus upon midrashic and allegorical interpretations of scripture

The text of Barnabas appears in numerous places among our collections of ancient manuscripts. Of these instances, there are two complete sources which are considered to be among the primary witnesses for the text:

1.2.1 Where did we get our text?

(a) Our oldest complete copy of the text of Barnabas is contained in **Codex Sinaiticus** (often indicated by the symbol ℵ). This fourth-century manuscript was discovered by the scholar Constantin von Tischendorf in 1844 at Saint Catherine's monastery on Mount Sinai. Here one can find both the Old (in part) and New Testaments, followed immediately thereafter by the texts of Barnabas and the Shepherd of Hermas. This manuscript, which has been identified with the Alexandrian textual tradition, suggests that Barnabas was somehow closely associated with manuscript preservation and research in ancient, Christian Egypt. Several later corrections have been made to the manuscript, perhaps from the seventh century.

(b) The second important copy of the text is the Greek version of Barnabas included in **Codex Hierosolymitanus** (previously known as Codex Constantinopolitanus). This **codex** was found in 1873 by Archbishop Philotheos Bryennios of Nicomedia in the Holy Sepulcher Church of Constantinople (modern Istanbul). According to a note which has been preserved together with the **codex,** this copy was written by an otherwise unknown, eleventh-century scribe named Leo. The text has been dated to June 1056. Along with this copy of Barnabas, the manuscript contains a *Synopsis of the Holy Scriptures* that was compiled by **John Chrysostom,** the only complete text of the Didache and Greek versions of 1–2 Clement, the long form of the thirteen letters of Ignatius, and an explanation of the genealogy of Jesus. The text of Barnabas which appears here is very similar to that which appears in **Codex Sinaiticus,** as described above.

The text of Barnabas has been preserved in abbreviated forms elsewhere. Some of these forms are quite important to a clear understanding of the manuscript tradition. They include the following:

(c) Nine Greek texts contain a defective form of Barnabas which is attached to Polycarp's letter to the Philippians. As a result of some scribal error, in each instance the text of Polycarp 1–9 is followed immediately by Barnabas 5–21 without a break, suggesting that the entire work was attributed to the bishop Polycarp. The oldest example of the texts has been traced to the eleventh century. The whole of these manuscripts should undoubtedly be considered together as a family of witnesses, all of which stem from a single manuscript tradition.

(d) There is one Latin version of Barnabas which contains chapters 1–17 only. These chapters are somewhat abbreviated in form in comparison with the longer Greek witnesses. It is not clear whether this is the work of the scribe who translated the text from the Greek or, instead, represents a shortened Greek source itself.

This version was produced in the late second century and has been preserved for us by a ninth-century manuscript (Codex Corbeiensis) which is stored in St. Petersburg, Russia.

(e) In his well-known text of the *Stromateis*, **Clement of Alexandria** quotes at least seven times from Barnabas and uses similar materials upon numerous other occasions. The early church historian **Eusebius of Caesarea** observes that Clement also had written a commentary upon the text, although this work is now lost to us. Clement ascribed a certain scriptural authority to Barnabas and undoubtedly possessed a dependable manuscript version as a result of his close proximity to the famous library of Alexandria.

(f) Fragments of Barnabas 1.1, 19.1–2 and 8, and 20.1 have been preserved in the Syriac language. The value of such a small portion of the text is limited for the purposes of manuscript study.

(g) Some scholars have indicated that portions of the text of Barnabas (specifically 1.1; 19.2a and 9b; 21.2–4) were incorporated into the later Ethiopic *Apostolic Church Order*. While this is possible, it seems more likely that the *Apostolic Church Order* has used parallel materials which are preserved in Didache 1–6.

(h) Barnabas 18–20 contains the so-called Two Ways tradition, which reflects materials which are primarily Jewish in origin. The Two Ways concept was widely regarded throughout the ancient world, where it appears in parallel materials such as **Manual of Discipline** 3.13–4.26 from Qumran and Didache 1–6. Some common heritage is suggested, though it is difficult to trace a firm, historical relationship among these texts. In the case of the Didache early scholars once argued either that Barnabas 18–20 was drawn from Didache 1–6 or that the Didache was dependent upon Barnabas. Most recent authorities agree, however, that the two texts have borrowed from some common source.

The text of Barnabas is offered as a letter or, by virtue of its formal nature, one might refer to it as an epistle. In this respect the text contains all of the classic sections that characterized ancient letters. The reader finds here, for example, an introduction (1.1), a section of appreciation for the reader and the reason for writing (1.2–5), the body or main message of the author (1.6–17.2), a call for ethical behavior (18.1–20.2), and a closing greeting (21.1–9). Authors throughout antiquity utilized this standard letter form, as is illustrated in the letters of Paul in the New Testament.

1.2.2 What form does the text take?

The letter format in which the text of Barnabas currently appears, however, is not original. Instead, some unknown editor has fashioned the current letter by combining two separate literary sources, neither of which was itself a letter. A close examination of the text reveals the presence of the first source in chapters 1–17, which originally served as an ancient essay on the Old Testament scriptures. Most scholars believe that these chapters may even preserve an early form of a homily or sermon. Chapters 18–20 come from a separate tradition, on the other hand, and contain materials associated with the well-known Two Ways pattern of instruction or code of conduct. This form of instruction was commonly used to teach Christians about what it meant to live an appropriate lifestyle. (For another example of this Two Ways pattern, the reader should consult the materials in Didache 1–6). Our author, or perhaps a later editor, joined these two sources and added words at either end of the text (1.1–5 and 21.1–9) to produce an extensive treatise within the framework of a letter.

In conformity with the letter format, Barnabas has been carefully crafted to include all of the typical elements of letters from the late first-century period. After the opening words of greeting and thanks for the presence of the spirit among the recipients, an extensive discussion arises around three elements of doctrine and belief—hope and faith, righteousness and judgment, joy and righteousness. These elements form the primary framework upon which selected Christian themes are raised and thereafter discussed. One might consider these materials to form the *statement* of the letter. In response to this discussion, the Two Ways materials that follow serve as a command to the audience to respond appropriately to the themes which have just been offered. One might say that these latter materials form the *charge* of the letter. The reader thus receives a statement of doctrine and faith and thereafter is charged to fulfill the requirements of that statement. In conclusion, the author offers final warnings and blessings to the readers. This pattern of elements appears throughout most letters from antiquity, both in the everyday letters between family members and in the correspondence between royal officials.

1.2.3 Who was the author?

The text offers no reliable clues with respect to the actual identity of its author. Of course, it is true that the name "Barnabas" appears at two places in certain manuscripts. The first occurs in the title that opens the text. Scholars generally think that this is a secondary addition, especially since ancient authors typically did not begin their manuscripts with titles—unlike modern authors. The second appearance occurs in the phrase "The Epistle of Barnabas," which is appended at the conclusion of the text. The tendency to conclude, rather than to begin, a manuscript with a title or **incipit** was common among most ancient texts. The position of the title here thus more authentically reflects ancient literary practices. The question remains, however, whether the use of the name "Barnabas" should be considered as authentic. If so, to whom does the name refer?

Several early Christian writers, including the scholar **Jerome** (in Rome) and both **Clement of Alexandria** and **Serapion of Thmuis** (in Egypt), believed that the author of the text was the apostle Barnabas. We know about Barnabas from the writings of the New Testament, where he is named in Acts 11–15 and Galatians 2 as an early Christian evangelist who accompanied the apostle Paul on the first of his four missionary journeys around the Mediterranean world. Few scholars continue to hold this view today, however, for two primary reasons. The late date of the text suggests that it was almost certainly written after the death of the apostle. Furthermore, the decidedly anti-Jewish tone of the materials would not seem to support its having been written by someone who came from a Jewish background, as did the apostle Barnabas. There are, of course, other ways of explaining the presence of the name, Barnabas.

(a) The author may actually have been named Barnabas, but was someone different from the apostle known from the New Testament. This option is the least likely, primarily since the name is neither widely attested within the ancient church nor often used as a source of authority within early literary traditions.

(b) The letter is a **pseudepigraph,** that is, the author offered the text under the identity of the apostle in order to gain some greater authority for the writing. This practice was widespread among ancient authors who often used the names of great persons either to honor a prominent figure from some historical tradition or to gain acceptance for materials which were believed to be a close reflection of that person's thought. This is certainly a strong possibility which should not be discounted.

(c) The letter was written anonymously and only later was independently attributed to the apostle Barnabas, most likely in order to lend some apostolic legitimacy to the writing. As with the second option above, this too is possible and bears equal credibility.

The question of authorship raises the need to define the term *author*. During the rise of the early church, the teachings of important persons and traditions were transmitted both in oral forms and in various written texts. While it is almost certain that much of the material in our work is specifically from a single person, it also is undoubtedly true that the text reflects numerous ancient sources which have been collected to form the basis of the larger document. Our so-called author, therefore, may perhaps be better described by modern standards as a collector or editor. In this respect the person who fashioned the text may be reflected best in the general theology of the work and less so in those sources from which the text borrows.

Apart from the name "Barnabas," we know nothing about the occupation and status of the author. It is fair to say that the author was respected within the boundaries of the local church, primarily because the text's broad selection of materials is delivered with an assumption of leadership. At the same time the precise position of authority from which the writing is given remains obscure. Is this a church elder from a neighboring community? Is this an itinerant teacher without any specific home? Is this a leader in the community whose homily or sermon comes from a position of local honor and authority? While there is no consensus on the answer to such questions, this last perspective is the most widely endorsed among scholars today.

Unfortunately, though no definitive answer to the question of authorship is possible, the text suggests that the author (or editor) was a second- or third-generation Christian—not one of the early apostles of the church. In all likelihood this person did not come from a strongly Jewish background. At a later time another person, one who may not even have known the actual identity of the author, borrowed the name of the Jewish apostle Barnabas and applied it to the text in order to gain a broader acceptance for the writing.

1.2.4 When was the text written?

As with the question of authorship, it is difficult to know exactly when the text was written. With respect to the issue of date, however, there are more clues to consider in the discussion. It appears likely that the letter could not have been composed before AD 70. This is supported by the reference in chapter 16 to the destruction of the temple in Jerusalem. The texts supporting this reference have been borrowed from the Old Testament text of Isaiah, which itself alludes to the earlier destruction of the temple by the Babylonians in the sixth century BC. Undoubtedly, though, this text has been applied here within the fresh context of the war of AD 66–70 between the Jews and Rome, which concluded with the destruction of the temple.

It is also widely recognized that by the third century **Clement of Alexandria** knew this letter well and even endorsed it as scripture. The letter must therefore have gained some authority and obtained wide circulation prior to this time, which roughly represents the final years of Clement's career.

Within these parameters there are three primary theories:

(a) Some scholars believe that the letter should be attributed to the years 70–79. This date is often linked to a passage in chapter 4 based upon the Old Testament book of Daniel that speaks of the rise and reign of ten worldly kingdoms. Presumably the author of Barnabas connected these kingdoms with particular empires in antiquity, much as Revelation 17 does in the New Testament. To assign the letter to these years would provide a proper context for the view that the apostle Barnabas was the actual author.

(b) A more recent, and the most widely supported, theory places the date of composition during the years AD 96–100. This view proposes that both the theological perspectives and historical data within the text indicate a date closer to the end of the first century, or even to the beginning of the second century. Scholars endorsing this perspective favor a date within the reign of the Roman emperor **Nerva** (96–98) or during the opening years of his successor, **Trajan**. Both emperors' attitude toward the growth and spread of Christianity was less hostile than that of their predecessors.

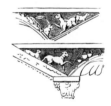

(c) The remaining theory dates the letter to approximately 132–135. This perspective centers once again upon the status of the temple, specifically upon the allusion to its reconstruction in Barnabas 16. Though the text depends upon the imagery of the prophet Isaiah, the allusion may have been employed as a reference to any of the various limited attempts to reconstruct the temple occurring between AD 70–131; after that the entire temple precinct was ultimately destroyed during the second war of the Jews with Rome in 132–135.

Since the evidence is not conclusive for any of these options, it is wise to choose the more moderate opinion which places the writing at the end of the first century. The historical features of the text are consistent with this period in the growth of the early church. Moreover the stylistic approach and theological concerns of the author are consistent with other contemporary writings, such as the Didache and the letters of Ignatius from the apostolic fathers, as well as the books of Hebrews and Revelation from the New Testament.

1.2.5 In what setting was the text written?

Scholars concur that the text originated in or around the Egyptian city of Alexandria, the second largest city in the Roman Empire. The strongest supporting evidence for this theory is that the Letter of Barnabas had its widest acceptance and use in this area. As stated above, **Clement of Alexandria,** an eminent theologian and scripture scholar in early Christian Egypt, considered this text to bear the authority of scripture. Clement's student **Origen** likewise conferred the status of scripture upon the text and referred to it as a "catholic" (or universally acknowledged) epistle. Perhaps surprisingly, the fourth-century bishop **Athanasius,** who also was associated with the church in Alexandria, did not include the text in his list of authoritative writings. Finally, the letter was copied into an important biblical manuscript of the general region, **Codex Sinaiticus.** This **codex** places it and the Shepherd of Hermas immediately after the book of Revelation as an apocalyptic conclusion to the entire collection of early Christian scripture.

An additional piece of evidence that supports the association of the text with the region of Alexandria is the heavy dependence of Barnabas on that approach to scriptural interpretation known as the **allegorical method**—the view that scripture holds a deeper meaning than that which is immediately apparent from a literal reading of the text. The search for allegories in scripture was widely practiced within the large school of Jewish scripture scholars in Alexandria. As illustrated in the work of the Jewish author **Philo,** it was in Alexandria that Jewish theology explored the allegories of scripture as a means of confronting the philosophical challenges of Greek culture. One might consider it to be only natural, therefore, that the allegorical approach to scripture that dominated the work of Jewish scholars in the city should influence early Christian theologians there as well, including both **Clement** and **Origen,** and presumably the author of Barnabas.

A final piece of evidence in support of Alexandria is the author's emphasis upon the concept of *gnōsis*. This Greek term is usually translated as "knowledge" and suggests a special understanding of life. One of the main purposes of the Letter of Barnabas is to share with the reader this true, secret knowledge of Christianity. Egyptian scholars were widely recognized for their emphasis upon the element of knowledge within Christian theology, so the environs of Alexandria became one of the homes for the early gnostic movement, or **gnosticism,** which gained a wide following within ancient Christianity. While the emphasis upon knowledge as a key to religious understanding was by no means limited to the Alexandrian area, its pervasive presence in the writings of authors from that city seems to recommend the hypothesis of an Alexandrian origin for the text.

According to the author, the text of Barnabas was written for its readers "in order that, together with your faith, you might have perfect knowledge" (1.5). This "knowledge" to which the author makes reference appears to take the form of three so-called *doctrines* or concepts—hope of life, righteousness, and love of joy and happiness—recurring throughout chapters 1–17 as the hinges upon which the text was constructed. These ideas may be summarized briefly:

1.2.6 Why was the text written?

(a) The "hope of life" exists for each Christian within the specific faith of that individual believer. This idea is explained in the discussion in 2.1–4.5. Here the reader is admonished to hold certain, correct Christian virtues, to make the appropriate personal sacrifice toward God, to participate in fasting with honest integrity, and to be assured that God's reward for Christian hope will arrive in the near future.

(b) The doctrine of "righteousness" follows next in the discussion in 4.6–12.11. The early Christian concept of righteousness assumed the setting of the ancient lawcourt. That person who was found to be righteous was, in some sense, someone who had been determined by an appropriate judge to be innocent. With respect to Christian faith, our text assumes that the label of righteousness can be awarded to any faithful believer who has withstood the divine judgment of God. The author observes that Israel, which lost its covenant promise because of its lack of obedience to God's ways, subsequently was not found to be righteous according to divine judgment. For this reason God revealed Christ to all nations through the death of Jesus of Nazareth upon the cross. The reality of this event was foretold by those great figures of the Old Testament who called for faith and obedience to God and who anticipated the imagery of the cross and baptism throughout their prophecies.

(c) Finally, the "love of joy and happiness" stands as a witness to the fact that any particular believer has indeed obtained righteousness in the sight of God. Chapters 13–16, which contain the discussion of this idea, emphasize that the joy of Christians is justified by their claim to be the true heirs of the covenant of Christ, an idea symbolized by the establishment of a new sabbath and a new temple, or a new day and place for the worship of God.

An essential aspect of chapters 1–17 is the focus on what the author perceives to be the *correct* interpretation of the Old Testament scriptures. The goal of this interpretation is to illustrate that the scriptures have always spoken of and anticipated the coming of the messiah who would bring salvation to the world and be the complete revelation of God to humanity. The author of Barnabas insists that this interpretation is not *a* correct way to interpret the scriptures but, instead, is *the* way. Further, the author argues that the Jews have failed to understand the pronouncements of God properly in this respect. Consequently, the Jews are thought to have rejected the Old Testament covenant when it was given to Moses by God at Mount Sinai. A similar desire to distinguish the early Christian faith from its roots in Judaism is typical of late first-century and early second-century Christian writings, much as one finds in the claims of the Gospel of John in the New Testament. Such arguments reveal the difficult situation of an emerging theology which sought to justify its precarious situation among the religions of the Roman Empire through a fresh and novel use of the Old Testament—the traditional, sacred writings of Judaism.

Although the final part of Barnabas (chapters 18–20, and perhaps 21) originally contained no concern for the three doctrines of knowledge, these materials have been added to chapters 1–17 to reinforce the doctrines. The goal of these final chapters is to contrast the dual pathways of light and darkness. In this process the author first lists a number of characteristics present in the life of the person walking in the way of light: humility, faithfulness, truthfulness, modesty, etc. Next, one finds traits of those who walk in the way of darkness: idolatry, arrogance, hypocrisy, pride, etc. The original concern of these materials undoubtedly was to offer a model of ethical behavior which was to guide the lifestyle of Christians. In their current position these materials serve a similar, though more specific, function: to illustrate an ethical pattern for daily life which is demanded by the message of the three doctrines in the previous chapters.

The place of Christianity among the various religions of the Roman Empire at the end of the first century was tenuous at best. The young Christian movement was only one among numerous philosophies and faiths competing for the attention of peoples around the Mediterranean world. Our author was concerned to reassure his readers that their hopes and expectations with respect to the claims of Christianity were in fact justified. To this end the text utilizes some specific tools in its efforts to encourage the early church: a concern to redefine the faith, history, and symbols of Judaism; an effort to employ the promise of the end times as a catalyst for faith; and a desire to explain the special knowledge that is inherent to Christianity.

1.2.7 What are the primary traits of the text?

(a) Redefinition of Judaism. The single religious tradition onto which the author attached the claims of Christianity is the faith of Israel, or Judaism. On the one hand, Judaism was one of the few religions within the Roman Empire officially sanctioned by Roman law. On the other, the traditions of Judaism were widely known throughout the Mediterranean world and held claim to an ancient history of belief. The author thus chose to employ the history and traditions of Judaism as a foundation stone upon which to build the new claims of emerging Christianity.

The argument of Barnabas, in essence, is formulated upon the view that God had previously chosen the people of Israel (the Jews) to share in a covenant of salvation. In the revelation of this covenant throughout history, Israel's leaders foretold the coming of God's ultimate reign. This prophecy evoked the symbols of a purity of lifestyle and thought, participation in cleansing baptism, and the sacrifice of God's own son upon the cross. Scripture records the witness of Abraham, Isaac, Jacob, David, the prophets, and even Moses to this vision of the future. Yet the people of Israel were blind to this promise and through disobedience lost their claim to the covenant. Now, according to this witness and the more recent testimony of the apostles of Jesus of Nazareth, this covenant has been made available to all peoples who will believe in its promises. The old institutions and rituals of Judaism have been redefined into new images of understanding about the relationship of God to those who accept this covenant. In this effort, the numerous images of the Old Testament writings have been carefully manipulated by means of the **allegorical method** to apply to the current situation of the early church.

(b) The promise of the end times (or **eschatology**). Our author emphasizes the rapidly approaching end of time and the resulting urgency for individual faith in response to that moment. This concern is evident in the underlying assumption that all people of the covenant faith, in alignment with God, constantly struggle in opposition to "the Black One" (4.9; 20.1) and his followers. Yet this struggle ensues with the understanding that the promise of ultimate victory does indeed rest with God. This critical premise underlies the numerous ideas of chapters 1–17 and is driven by a form of cosmic **dualism,** that is, the view that the activities of the world are divided between two primary forces—good and evil. Even the concluding chapters of the text (chapters 18–20), which bring an ethical dimension to this belief, insist that the paths of light and darkness are ruled by *angels* who are associated with these forces. As with the **Manual of Discipline** (from Qumran), these angels are under the influence of good and evil respectively. The author insists that the Jews were previously deceived by an evil spirit and, hence, have been led into disobedience against God. While it is not explicitly stated as such, the reader is to assume that the Jews have been steered by an evil spirit into the way of darkness.

In one of the more intriguing portions of the text, chapter 4, the author anticipates a forthcoming crisis within world history which is referred to as the "final scandal." Here materials from the **apocalyptic literature** of Daniel in the Old Testament (a basis for the book of Revelation in the New Testament as well) trace the rise of "ten wicked kingdoms" in history and the evil beast that will seek to subdue those who have faith in God. The text of Barnabas concludes with a reminder that the final outcome of history will see God as a victorious conqueror. This theme is constantly used both to encourage readers toward vigilance in their chosen course of faith and to motivate those who have not yet decided which path may be better to follow.

(c) Special knowledge. As mentioned above, the theme of knowledge *(gnōsis)* plays a prominent role throughout the text of Barnabas. Because the early church was rooted in Judaism, it searched the Hebrew Scriptures (or Old Testament) for those passages which explained and predicted the coming of Christ in the life and works of

Jesus. As long as the church was viewed by Roman law as a formal religious sect within Judaism, the rise of Christianity was legally secure. But as the followers of Christ were forced away from Judaism's centers of worship (the synagogues), the status of the new religious faith was endangered. Thus, two groups of people which used the same scriptures to justify their relationship with God came to very different conclusions about what those texts implied. The author of Barnabas sought to show that Christianity alone was able to perceive the true knowledge of God's promises within the Hebrew Scriptures, while Judaism had failed in this task and had rejected the words of Jesus and his apostles.

The concern for knowledge in our text raises the broader issue of **gnosticism** within the early church. **Gnosticism,** the belief that there is a secret knowledge which leads to salvation and is available only to select persons, was a focus of debate among early Christian authors; ultimately the later orthodox church condemned it as heretical. Some scholars have asked whether the text of Barnabas was not itself a form of early Christian **gnosticism.** While today one may reject some of the conclusions in the text, especially with regard to the text's harsh tone and the author's use of scripture to defend the Christian faith against Judaism, it would be best not to classify this document among the works of later so-called heresies within the Christian tradition. As the author explains in 17.2, there is yet even more wisdom to be offered about the future, though such wisdom is difficult to understand because this knowledge is contained in parables. In some sense the text of Barnabas is actually an early precursor to the stream of scriptural interpretation in Alexandria and to the trajectory of theological diversity in early Christian Egypt which made this geographical region appear to be doctrinally suspect, especially to the later orthodox church in western Europe. In the mind of our author, however, this knowledge is not so much restricted to a limited number of select persons, since it is available to all who will share the author's faith.

The author intends to illustrate how the entirety of the Old Testament scriptures refers to Christ. Chapters 1–17 focus upon biblical images and theological explanations illustrating the connection between Christ and the biblical tradition. Some of these connections appear to be straightforward, while others do not. Although the text of Barnabas is replete with such images, the following

1.2.8 What special images appear?

examples appear at the heart of our text and are particularly illustrative of the author's approach:

(a) The scapegoat (7.6–11). This image is taken from the acts of **atonement** that were offered on behalf of the people of Israel by their priest Aaron in Leviticus 16. In this passage two goats are selected: one to be sacrificed to God for the sins of the people; the other is to be released into the wilderness for Azazel, a widely recognized demon of the desert. Before the latter goat was sent forth the Israelites were to perform a ritual of **atonement** over it. This ritual included the placement of hands upon the head of the goat, at which time all of the sins of the people were confessed. Through this means the sins of Israel were cast out of the community.

Using the **allegorical method** our author reconfigures the imagery of the Old Testament text into a decidedly Christian understanding. By this means the special knowledge of faith in regard to this passage is shared with the reader. In this instance, for example, the author associates the second goat with the rejection of Jesus by the Jews. Jesus thus is portrayed as having taken upon himself the sins of the world, ultimately being handed over to the power of death. According to the author in 8.7, the moral to this episode is that those persons who see Jesus as the messiah and wish to enter the reign of God must accept his pain and suffering as their own.

(b) The red heifer (8.1–7). The image of the heifer is taken from Numbers 19:1–10. In this passage the God of Israel prescribes a law to Moses and Aaron on behalf of the people of Israel during their wandering journey in the Sinai desert. Here Israel was called upon to find a young heifer without defects, which was to become a sacrifice for the sins of Israel. Once the heifer had been sacrificed, its blood was sprinkled in the direction of the tent of meeting—the place of worship for the wandering Israelites—and the carcass then was ritually burned. Three men were involved in the ceremony—the priest, the man who burned the sacrificed heifer, and the man who gathered its ashes, which were to be used later.

As with the scapegoat imagery above, our author equates the heifer with Jesus by whose blood all Christians receive their salvation. The wood for the fire is said to represent the cross, and the (twelve) boys who sprinkled the blood upon the tent symbolize the twelve apostles who formerly preached the power of the gospel. The employment of such imagery as a basis for Christian theology was common in late first-century Christian literature, as is illustrated by a similar use of the scapegoat and heifer motifs in Hebrews 8–9 in the New Testament. The author of Barnabas has noted with special care, however, that through such imagery the vague commandments of the scriptures may be plainly understood with the knowledge of faith alone but remain obscure to those who ignore this approach.

(c) Jesus revealed in the circumcision of Abraham and his servants (9.7–9). Of particular interest here is an early Christian concern for **numerology**—the theory of interpretation that asserts that numbers are significant for theological understanding. With this image our author combines the number of Abraham's household (318 men, Genesis 14:14) together with a passage on circumcision (Genesis 17). For our author, Jesus thus is revealed in the number 318. In most ancient languages, as with the Greek language of our text, numbers are represented by letters. The Greek letter for the numeral 300 is equivalent to the English *T*, which the author believed to signify the cross of Jesus. The numeral 18 was composed of 10 and 8, which in Greek is formed by the letters I and H respectively. The letters IH became significant for our text, since they form the first two letters of the name of Jesus in Greek (= ΙΗΣΟΥΣ), and thus may be perceived as an abbreviation for that name. When these three letters were subsequently combined together (318 = T + IH), the author of Barnabas could argue that the reader now has been provided with the name of Jesus as it was revealed in connection with the cross—an important symbol of Christian theology indeed.

1.2.9 How does the text relate to scripture?

The relationship of Barnabas to the biblical tradition and to New Testament Christianity in general is not entirely clear, though certain outstanding elements may be discerned. The most striking, and perhaps surprising, aspect of the letter's relationship with the early church is that the text itself was considered to be scripture by many important theologians. This held especially true within the early Egyptian church, where the text was accepted as scripture by scholars who worked in the region of Alexandria and eventually was included in the **Codex Sinaiticus** version of the Bible. This reveals the indisputable respect which ancient church theologians held for the writing, though once again it must be quickly added that this appreciation was primarily regional. There are no additional references to the text outside of the Alexandrian area during the second and third centuries. As time progressed, the geographical area in which Barnabas was known slowly expanded, though the influence and importance of the writing simultaneously decreased.

As observed above, a most important feature of the text is the way in which it treats Old Testament scripture. In many respects the letter resembles much of the literature in the New Testament. Not least of these similarities is the frequent reference to the "Law and Prophets" of Jewish tradition. Our author uses these references to explain the role and person of Jesus in much the same way as the writers of the New Testament Gospels and Epistles. While it is only upon a limited number of occasions that our text reflects any specific New Testament materials themselves, many of its themes and ideas are similar.

The question of biblical associations ultimately raises the issue of what sources lie behind the text of Barnabas. This question may be answered best once we have divided the text into its two primary sections:

(a) As stated above, chapters 1–17 utilize numerous Old Testament texts. How these texts have been collected is particularly interesting. It is not unusual for Barnabas to begin a quote from the writings of the Prophets and then to attach two or more distinct passages from other biblical writings or from the Old Testament **Apocrypha** without indicating a change of sources. Also, the author of Barnabas seldom identifies any specific prophet, though it probably should be assumed that the first-century reader was able to determine the text in question. This certainly was a convenient means by which the author could quote from many different prophetic writings. At the same time, there appears to be yet another reason for this approach.

Many scholars believe that the author utilized short collections of texts which we now identify as **testimonia.** These collections formed short documents which contained many scriptural citations that often were associated with a common theme. It is presumed that such documents circulated widely in both Jewish and Christian circles during the early period of the church, as is illustrated by their presence in the writings of **Cyprian** and **Gregory of Nyssa.** As a resource, such collections permitted the essential teachings of Christian theology to be easily transmitted. Furthermore, these collections were a ready source of support for the composition of sermons and homilies.

Figure 1-A —POSSIBLE TESTIMONIA IN BARNABAS (ESPECIALLY FROM GENESIS, PSALMS, AND ISAIAH)

Image	Barnabas	Old Testament Allusions
Sacrifice	2.4–10	Isaiah 1:11–13; Jeremiah 7:22–23; Zechariah 8:17; Psalm 51:17
The stone	6.2–4	Isaiah 28:16; Isaiah 8:14; Isaiah 50:7; Psalm 118:22, 24
Circumcision	9.1–5	Psalm 18:44; Isaiah 33:13; Jeremiah 4:4; Jeremiah 7:2–3; Psalm 33:13; Isaiah 1:2, 10; Isaiah 40:3; Jeremiah 4:3–4; Deuteronomy 10:16; Jeremiah 9:25–26
Son of David	12.10–11	Psalm 110:1; Isaiah 45:1
The heir(s)	13.1–7	Genesis 25:12–23; Genesis 48:9; Genesis 48:13–19; Genesis 15:6; Genesis 17:4–5
Sabbath	15.1–9	Psalm 24:3–4; Jeremiah 17:24–25; Genesis 2:2; Psalm 90:4; Genesis 2:2; Psalm 24:4; Isaiah 1:13; Psalm 24:4

Another basis for the belief that **testimonia** contributed to the composition of Barnabas is the presence of peculiarities in some of the quotations. Scholars have attempted to identify the source of these quotations, both with reference to the prophet in question and with respect to the particular manuscript traditions behind the text. On the latter issue the text of Barnabas offers some problems. It is unclear, for instance, whether the majority of quotations were derived from the Hebrew version of the scriptures or from the Greek version (the **Septuagint**). On the one hand, it is entirely possible that our author borrowed from different versions of scripture. But the idea that the author used **testimonia** as a resource would better explain some of these peculiarities.

Finally, the author approaches the Old Testament through a specific form of textual interpretation known as **midrash**. This approach, used commonly among Jewish scholars, offers a unique blend of scriptural citations and theological explanations, typically with little or no regard for the historical circumstances of the texts' composition. New revelations quickly arose for interpreters who combined various scriptural texts on the basis of key words shared by those texts and then extracted *hidden* interpretations from these new combinations. The **allegorical method** employed in Barnabas was uniquely suited to this approach to scripture. As such, the way in which our author used texts is deeply reminiscent of later work among the scripture scholars of ancient Alexandria, both Jewish and non-Jewish.

(b) As seen above, the Two Ways motif behind chapters 18–20 reflects a common, early Christian tradition that served as a primary foundation for the author of the Didache as well. The Two Ways tradition appeared to be a conscious reflection of the **decalogue** of Exodus and Deuteronomy, though the unique approaches to scripture undertaken in chapters 1–17 were not applied to these texts. It is assumed that the addition of the Two Ways tradition to the materials of chapters 1–17 was undertaken primarily to provide an ethical reinforcement for the arguments of these chapters. Presumably, the mere presence of materials from the **decalogue** of Exodus and Deuteronomy was seen as adequate for this purpose without any need to employ the interpretation of **midrash** or the **allegorical method.**

1.3 CONTENTS

Outline of the Materials

Greetings! I am grateful for God's spirit which is in you. And now I write to complete your faith with knowledge.

There are three great doctrines from the Lord: the hope of life; righteousness; and the love of joy and happiness. Seek these truths, since the current days are precarious. The prophets of scripture revealed that cultic sacrifices and fasting are not of real value. Instead, a person's inward sacrifice and service to the oppressed are to be desired. In these final days we should seek God's laws and keep from evil.

The covenant of salvation was abandoned by Israel, and now it is ours alone. So let us be deserving in spirit, avoiding wicked ways and keeping God's commandments, in order to be judged as those who deserve salvation. It was for this reason that the Lord was crucified—for forgiveness of our sins. Those who know this and yet stray deserve to perish. The prophets foresaw this, and the apostles proclaimed it. Thus the Lord has become our foundation stone against which the Jews protest in vain. They lack the wisdom to recognize this creation of a new Israel—the Lord's new people of faith—who soon will receive the promises that were made to the patriarchs. Indeed, the last shall be first!

Clearly the many images of Moses and the prophets served as metaphors for us in order to foretell the suffering and death of Jesus, to assure our salvation through the circumcision of our hearts, and to warn us to avoid ungodly persons. And often these same figures alluded to the elements of baptism and crucifixion—symbols of that covenant which once before was rejected by Israel and now is offered

Summary of the Argument

to the nations. This is our promise of hope for that day when the wicked shall perish and we shall be made holy. In the same way that the physical temple in Jerusalem was destroyed, so the spiritual temple which has been constructed within us has been built for the Lord. I trust that with my words you can now understand all of these parables of salvation.

Finally, there are two great paths—one leads to light and the other to darkness. The first path requires that one love and glorify God, as well as avoid godless persons. Keep from all evil ways, follow the commandments of God, and maintain a proper household. Share with your neighbor, both as you give to the needy individual and as you contribute to the life of the community. Hate evil and pray with a clean conscience. As for the path of darkness, it is full of evil actions and thoughts, all of which are counter to the way of light. The believer must follow the ordinances of the Lord in order to be glorified in God's reign. This is the reason for the resurrection and the divine judgment.

Leaders, the end is near and the reward is close by! Counsel faithfully and in wisdom. May the Lord be with you.

1.4 RELATED LITERATURE

Andry, Carl F. "Introduction to the Epistle of Barnabas." Th.D. dissertation. Harvard University, 1950.

Barnard, L. W. "Is the Epistle of Barnabas a Paschal Homily?" In *Studies in the Apostolic Fathers and their Background.* Pages 73–85. New York: Schocken, 1966. (BQ1080.B366 1966)

_____. "The Problem of the Epistle of Barnabas." *Church Quarterly Review* 159 (3, 1958), pp. 211–30.

_____. "The Use of Testimonies in the Early Church and in the Epistle of Barnabas." In *Studies in the Apostolic Fathers and their Background.* Pages 109–35. New York: Schocken, 1966. (BQ1080.B366 1966)

Gunther, J. J. "The Epistle of Barnabas and the Final Rebuilding of the Temple." *Journal for the Study of Judaism* 7 (2, 1976), pp. 143–51.

Kraft, Robert A. *Barnabas and the Didache.* The Apostolic Fathers 3. New York: Thomas Nelson & Sons, 1965. (BQ1080.A4 1964)

Lowy, S. "The Confutation of Judaism in the Epistle of Barnabas." *Journal of Jewish Studies* 11 (1, 1960), pp. 1–33.

Muilenburg, James. *The Literary Relations of the Epistle of Barnabas and the Teaching of the Twelve Apostles.* Ph.D. dissertation. Yale University, 1926. Marburg, 1929. (BS2900.B3.M8 1926)

Robinson, J. A. *Barnabas, Hermas and the Didache.* London: S.P.C.K.; New York: Macmillan, 1920. (BQ172.R6 1920)

_____. "The Epistle of Barnabas and the Didache." *Journal of Theological Studies* 35 (2, 1934), pp. 113–46.

2 The Teaching of the Twelve Apostles (The Didache)

2.1 ANSWERS

2.1.1 Manuscript tradition—one Greek text (complete); one Greek fragment (1.3b–4a; 2.7b–3.2a); one Coptic text (10.3b–12.1a); one reported Georgian text (complete); portions in later writings; other parallels to Two Ways tradition (1.1–6.1)

2.1.2 Literary form—early church manual of instruction

2.1.3 Authorship—unknown Jewish Christian (perhaps several authors or editors)

2.1.4 Date—AD 70–150 (probably AD 80–120)

2.1.5 Setting—Syria (probably Antioch); possibly region of Palestine or Egypt

2.1.6 Purpose—to provide specific Christian instruction (for use by community leaders)

2.1.7 Primary elements—low Christology; regulations for baptism and thanksgiving (or eucharist); directions for church structure

2.1.8 Special images—two-tiered hierarchy; use of trinitarian formula; the holy vine of David; broken bread; a worldly mystery of the church

2.1.9 Relationship to scripture—primary focus upon Old Testament wisdom traditions; dependence upon sayings of Jesus; likely connection with Gospel of Matthew

2.2 QUESTIONS

2.2.1 Where did we get our text?

From about the fourth century AD, certain early Christian writers such as **Athanasius** in Alexandria, and shortly thereafter **Eusebius of Caesarea,** mentioned a writing commonly known as The Teaching of the (Twelve) Apostles. Today scholars typically refer to this work by the shortened title "Didache," a Greek word which means *teaching*. Very few copies of the Didache have survived from antiquity, and all but one are fragmentary.

(a) The first and most important copy of the text was discovered in 1873 by Archbishop Philotheos Bryennios of Nicomedia in the Holy Sepulcher Church of Constantinople (modern Istanbul). This version of the Didache appears in the eleventh-century **Codex Hierosolymi-tanus,** together with a text which is known as the *Synopsis of the Holy Scriptures* by **John Chrysostom,** the Letter of Barnabas, our only complete texts of 1–2 Clement in Greek, the so-called long version of the thirteen letters of Ignatius, and an explanation of the genealogy of Jesus. This is the only manuscript appearing to contain the entire text of the Didache and, even here, numerous scholars think that several lines may be lost from the end of this particular rendition.

Parts of the Didache have been preserved elsewhere in various fragmentary manuscripts:

(b) The first of these, a brief Greek fragment discovered in Oxyrhynchus, Egypt, was published in 1922. The text, known today as Oxyrhynchus Papyrus 1782, preserves sixty-four words from the Didache, specifically the materials at 1.3b–4a and 2.7b–3.2a. This short section probably comes from an early Christian book, or **codex,** and has been dated to the late fourth century. It is possible that this particular fragment was worn around the neck as an amulet to repel evil spirits.

(c) The second fragment appears in the late Egyptian language of Coptic and includes materials from 10.3b–12.1a. The text, known today as British Library Oriental Manuscript 9271, appears in two columns on one side of a single papyrus page, and concludes in a partial column on the reverse side. While some scholars believe that this text was designed to be a replacement page for an early **codex,** others believe that it represents a form of the Didache different from that in the primary Greek version above. The text dates to the fifth century.

In 1932 a complete version of the Didache was identified in the Georgian language, a dialect prevalent in the southern Caucasus region of eastern Europe. This nineteenth-century manuscript, which may represent a fifth-century translation, was found in Constantinople. Unfortunately it was never published and subsequently has been lost. Comparisons with the primary Greek version reportedly revealed only minor variations between the two texts, with the omission of the materials in 1.5–6 and 13.5–7 from the Georgian manuscript.

Portions of the Didache have been incorporated into several other early Christian texts. These texts offer examples of the ways in which the later church applied the teachings of the Didache to contemporary concerns and problems. For the most part, the Didache became widely recognized as useful for instructing community members and leaders. Two examples of this secondary usage of the Didache are the following:

(d) Book 7 of the fourth-century, Greek *Apostolic Constitutions* includes the majority of the Didache, though the text has generally been integrated into a broader context in order to meet the immediate needs of the editor.

(e) Section 52 of the Ethiopic church manual known as the *Apostolic Church Order* contains Didache 11.3–13.7 (minus 11.6 and 13.2), followed thereafter by 8.1–2a. The insertion of these materials diverges from the earlier Coptic and Arabic versions of the text.

The first part of the Didache, which contains the so-called Two Ways tradition (1.1–6.1), is also scattered among several other early manuscripts. These materials are primarily Jewish in origin, though the concept of Two Ways was widely recognized and taught throughout the ancient world. It is difficult to know how these various materials interrelated or whether any particular text was directly dependent upon the Didache itself, but some common heritage certainly is suggested. Examples of the Two Ways tradition that may be related to the Didache in some form or fashion include the following:

(f) Barnabas 18–20. While early scholars argued either that Didache 1–6 drew from Barnabas 18–20 or that Barnabas depended upon the Didache, most recent authorities agree that the two texts borrowed from some common source that has since been lost.

(g) The Latin *Apostolic Teaching* (often called by its Latin title, the *Doctrina Apostolorum*). The *Teaching* is known from two textual witnesses—a fragmentary ninth/tenth-century text containing parallels to 1.1–3a and 2.2–6a only, and an eleventh-century text that includes 1.1–3a and 2.2–6.1. Scholars disagree as to whether this version relies upon a Jewish form of the Two Ways that was independent of the Didache or, instead, whether the text is some form of homily that incorporated both the Didache and Barnabas.

(h) The Arabic *Life of Shenoute*. This Egyptian text, which is an account of the life and teachings of the desert monk Shenoute, omits 1.3b–2.1 and abridges 5.1–2. It reveals an early interest in the teachings of the Didache by the Egyptian monastic tradition.

(i) The fourth-century *Summary of Doctrine* (often called by its Latin title, the *Syntagma Didascalias*). Perhaps written by the bishop

Athanasius in Egypt, this text only hints at a dependence upon the Didache.

(j) The *Rule of Benedict*. Section 4 of the *Rule,* a document containing the primary teachings of the monk Benedict, reveals a great dependence upon the Two Ways tradition and probably even upon the Didache itself.

The Didache generally is recognized as an early church manual that was used to instruct new candidates for a specific Christian community. Such instruction typically was offered to each candidate for church membership prior to baptism. Although the text maintains a basic literary unity, the divergent interests and approaches of the materials strongly suggest that more than one writer is at work here. It is even likely that a secondary editor has modified the text. Most likely the text was employed for various other purposes in the earliest stages of its composition. From the nature of the materials in the Didache and from its use in later works, however, it seems reasonable to assume that the final form of the text was employed for general instruction.

2.2.2 What form does the text take?

The current text of the Didache is traditionally divided by modern scholars into sixteen distinct chapters, which themselves can be split into two major divisions: chapters 1–6 (the Two Ways tradition) and chapters 7–15 (instructions on liturgy and church structure). Chapter 16, which contains apocalyptic materials, is variously included with either division at the discretion of individual scholars. Both of the major divisions include materials that undoubtedly come from among the most ancient of church traditions and reflect early Christian practices that were eventually altered or dropped by the later institutional church. In addition, each division contains materials that were probably added to the text at some later date, most likely as an attempt to incorporate the text into the developing mainstream of Christian tradition. Such materials are scattered throughout the whole of the Didache. The most widely acknowledged example of these interpolations appears in 1.3b–2.1; this material seems to have been compiled from an assortment of other early Jewish and Christian texts.

In the case of the Didache, it is particularly difficult to identify the author. In all likelihood several persons were involved in the composition and evolution of the text, but the nature of this process

2.2.3 Who was the author?

is unclear. For example, was there a single author who was followed by a later editor (or editors)? Did several authors contribute materials in some close historical sequence? Or did one editor perhaps combine numerous materials from the common Christian tradition into a single text with the addition of other comments and instructions (perhaps by yet another person)?

The title of the text offers no genuine help in identifying the author. Although the work is acknowledged to reflect early apostolic teachings, its title is generally thought to have been added much later, when the author and editors of the work had been forgotten.

The author of the Didache (typically called the "Didachist") is not identified in the text, nor does this person align with any particular tradition or school of thought. At first glance, therefore, it may appear that the author's identity was of no importance to the original recipients. It is much more likely, however, that the Didachist was well-known to the original readers and did not need any identification within the text. It thus falls upon the modern reader to identify the author by whatever evidence may be gleaned from the text itself.

It seems likely that the author was well-established within some early Christian setting, since many of the materials in the Didache are associated with traditional community concerns—ethical instruction, rules for liturgical rituals, the role of community officials. Throughout the text the instructions of the Didachist are consistently Jewish in tone and are rooted in traditional Old Testament writings and teachings. For example, chapters 2–3 are constructed upon an abbreviated form of the **decalogue.** Within chapter 3, the reader also is addressed as "my child"—a phrase which is typical of the Jewish wisdom tradition. Furthermore, while the author continually refers to "the Lord," there is a certain ambiguity about whether this reference is to God the Father or to Jesus as the Son of God. Indeed, the name of Jesus is used in the Didache only in liturgical formulas and is never identified specifically with the title of Christ (or messiah). Such details suggest that the Didachist was an early Jewish Christian whose religious perspective was still closely allied with the synagogue and with traditional Jewish beliefs.

To identify the author as an early Jewish Christian, however, is not to say much. Indeed, it may be that there was never a single individual who composed the document in a single session; rather, an initial author probably used a short form of the text to address an immediate issue in the community, and then subsequent editors added information to make the document relevant to other communities. That the perspective of these persons was profoundly Jewish is significant as a reflection of the theological world of the author and later editors.

2.2.4 When was the text written?

Modern scholarship has constantly debated over the date of the writing of the Didache. No absolute date is certain, though the broadest consensus of current thought would place the composition of the text in all of its various stages between AD 70 and 150. Certain sayings in chapters 1–6 and specific liturgical traditions in chapters 7–10 undoubtedly were composed and collected prior to 70, which is roughly the date of the composition of the Gospel of Mark. Yet it is unlikely that these materials were compiled into the first phase of the Didache prior to this period. At the same time, the literary style and approach of the text compare favorably to those of **Justin Martyr** and his student **Tatian,** both of whom wrote widely around the middle of the second century. One might safely assume that the text reached its final form by AD 150.

At the turn of the twentieth century some scholars theorized that the editor of the Didache was a follower of the Montanist sect. **Montanism** had gathered considerable attention by the late second century; it seemed reasonable to these scholars that the Didache was compiled during this general period, that is, no earlier than the late second or early third century and possibly as late as the fourth century. The already limited evidence for this theory is further weakened by the fact that the author of the fourth-century *Apostolic Constitutions,* who used the Didache as the basis for Book 7 of that text, already considered the Didache to be an ancient and renowned work. As a result, the "Montanist theory" no longer receives any wide support.

The present form of the Didache does not appear to have been written at a single point in time but evolved into the document we know today. Scholars are relatively certain that different parts of the text were added over the course of many years. It is most important, therefore, to offer a general framework of time for the earliest and latest editions of the text.

As for the earliest form of the text, Didache 1–6, which focuses upon the ancient Two Ways tradition, offers little evidence of the concerns of late first-century Christianity, but instead reflects a primitive understanding of Christian theology. The materials here could have been preserved from among the earliest texts and beliefs of the primitive Christian community, and in their oral form they could have circulated as early as the ministry of Paul, probably in the 50s. At the same time, the apocalyptic warnings of chapter 16 may be equally as old. Throughout the Didache, more recent sayings and traditions which seem to reflect some knowledge of the New Testament Gospels (ca. AD 70–90) have been introduced by later editors, but there is no reason to doubt that the bulk of materials in chapters 1–6 was written by the time of the writing of the gospels themselves. Further, the Two Ways tradition of the Didache parallels that of Barnabas 18–20. If, as many scholars believe, the Didachist and the author of Barnabas relied upon a common source for these materials, then this source must have been in wide circulation well before the end of the first century.

In chapters 7–15 the Didache also preserves what are most likely quite ancient traditions from the early church. Intermingled here, however, are traces of issues that help us to date the final edition of the text:

(a) Throughout, these chapters reflect the contemporary issues addressed by the author (or some secondary editor), who wished to speak to the community about the treatment of wandering prophets and the role of local, established authorities. We can infer from this material that the church still existed in a transitional period between the time of the wandering apostles and Christian prophets and the establishment of a hierarchical organization of governance. Since such a transition occurred quite naturally with the death of the original apostles and their immediate followers in the late first and early second centuries, these dates are suggested by the related texts.

(b) The letters of Ignatius of Antioch, which typically are dated around AD 110–120, argue extensively in favor of a single bishop for each church community; this bishop exercises authority over the positions of presbyters and deacons. Such church structure is not envisioned in the Didache, which mentions only bishops and deacons but not presbyters. It is unclear whether the Didache in fact represents a kind of two-tiered hierarchy among church communities that omits the role of presbyters, or perhaps is unconcerned for a single-bishop system of authority. We are led to believe, however, that the Didachist wrote in a period that had not yet felt the influence of Ignatius's view—again, the early second century.

(c) The author of the Didache appears to have some knowledge of the New Testament Gospel of Matthew, which is generally dated around AD 80–90. Cryptic references to "as you find in the gospel" as well as various traditions and sayings paralleling Matthew, suggest that the editor of the Didache in its final stages was aware of the Gospel of Matthew. The likelihood of this gospel's influence further suggests that the text's final edition was not constructed much before the end of the first century.

With this information in mind, scholars generally date the composition of the Didache somewhere between 80 and 120. During this period the earliest traditions of emerging Christianity were still available and useful to specific communities, while new problems of structure and authority had begun to raise serious issues for church leaders throughout the Roman Empire.

Several locations have been offered as possibilities for the place of origin, or provenance, of the Didache. Among these suggestions are the cities of Antioch, Caesarea, Jerusalem, and Pella. To this list one may also add some more general regions, such as Asia Minor, Egypt, Palestine, and Syria. The current scholarly consensus tends to divide between Egypt and Syria as the general region of origin.

2.2.5 In what setting was the text written?

Although widely endorsed by previous scholars, the region of Egypt perhaps holds the smaller share of opinion at present. Two factors favor Egypt as the provenance:

(a) Many materials and proposed sources which were used by the Didachist are reflected as well by Egyptian texts. The most notable of these sources, of course, is the Two Ways tradition which is paralleled in Barnabas 18–20. At the same time, the focus of the Didachist upon Old Testament materials and the Jewish perspective of early Christianity would have been at home in an area such as Alexandria, Egypt. Because Judaism continued to flourish in Alexandria into the third century, it undoubdtedly served as a primary influence upon the development of Christian theology.

(b) The majority of the later writings preserving materials from the Didache are in fact the products of Egypt. As an example, one may include here the Greek fragment of the Didache from Oxyrhynchus, the Coptic text of Didache 10–12, the *Apostolic Constitutions,* the *Apostolic Church Order,* and the *Life of Shenoute.* Arguments for the Egyptian origin of the Didache based upon geographical proximity are difficult to maintain, however, since in each instance it may be that the Didache, or some portion of it, could have held some special appeal for the church in Egypt. Further, it is generally true that much early Christian literature has been preserved because of the physical and cultural climate of Egypt. The heat and low humidity of the region are suitable for the preservation of ancient texts; moreover the Egyptian region enjoys a long tradition in which scholars have collected and preserved important documents.

As a more likely alternative to Egypt, the region of Syria, possibly even Antioch, probably should be considered as the favored location for the provenance of the Didache. This setting explains the possible association of the Didache with the Gospel of Matthew, or at least with the sources used by Matthew. Antioch, like Alexandria, was a city with a long tradition of Jewish literary and cultural influence upon its neighbors, not least of which was the early Christian community. Likewise, certain materials in the Didache, such as the prayers of thanksgiving (chapters 9–10) and the concern to abstain from ritually impure food (chapter 6), reflect issues and approaches that we know concerned communities of Syria and Asia Minor.

Some credit should be given to those theories of origin that envision the earliest form of the Didache as being produced in a Palestinian setting, possibly in Jerusalem. One might argue that the text was transferred to a Syrian setting, such as Antioch, where it was further adapted to the immediate situation of the Christians who lived there. This view assumes that the author and/or those who carried the text perhaps fled Jerusalem after the destruction of the city in the war between the Jews and Rome in 66–70 and the subsequent expulsion of Jews from the area (Christians along with them). The region of Antioch had maintained a strong Jewish community since the fourth century BC, so it would have been natural for displaced Jews (and Christians) to migrate to the city during this period of turmoil in Palestine. This reinforces the idea that Syria served in some fashion as a setting for the Didache.

2.2.6 Why was the text written?

The Didache is commonly thought to have been composed for general Christian instruction. Some scholars view the writing as perhaps the earliest example of an ancient church manual. Indeed, the Didache was often incorporated into later writings to serve this very purpose. Yet while it is helpful for the modern student to be able to assign the text to such a broad literary category, the composite nature of the work makes it likely that the Didache was used for a variety of purposes during the different stages of its active life.

The bulk of the Two Ways portion of the Didache (chapters 1–6), and perhaps the apocalyptic warnings at the end of the text (chapter 16), is undoubtedly drawn from ancient sources and probably represents the oldest layer of the text. Here the reader finds an exhortation to choose the *way of life* (as opposed to the *way of death*) as the basis for living the Christian faith. The use of such an exhortation in other early writings, such as in Barnabas and the **Manual of Discipline** (from Qumran), suggests that this theme was widely regarded in antiquity as a general call for correct living, not only among Jews and Christians but among other groups as well. It is quite likely that these materials, or the earliest form of the Didache, were used for the same purpose either within some specific Christian community or by the early church at large to serve as a model for general Christian instruction.

Whatever the exact origins of the Two Ways tradition, it eventually assumed a decidedly Christian tone in the Didache. This is aptly illustrated by the presence of two specific texts, 1.3b–2.1 and 6.1–2, which now are generally acknowledged as later additions. Originally the great teaching of the Two Ways in 1.1–2, that is, to love God and one's neighbor and to shun all manner of evil, was considered to be sufficiently illustrated by the teachings of the **decalogue** (or Ten Commandments) and by the traditional categories of the Jewish wisdom tradition which appear in chapters 2–5. With the insertion of 1.3b–2.1, these materials assumed a secondary role as illustrations of the Two Ways theme. They had been superseded by sayings attributed elsewhere to Jesus in the New Testament Gospels—to love one's enemies, to accept insult and abuse, and to give freely. Some scholars contend that this was a conscious attempt to replace the authority of traditional Jewish wisdom with the teachings of Jesus. At roughly the same time, the materials of 6.1–2, which charge the reader not to stray from the teaching of the Two Ways, shift the focus of the tradition away from general instruction about appropriate Christian ethics toward a new role as *the* correct teaching of the principles of God. In some manner these additions most likely were inserted into the text together with the addition of chapters 11–15. So too, the materials of chapter 16, which probably served as the original conclusion to the Two Ways materials of chapters 1–6, were likely shifted to the end of the newly expanded text to serve the general purpose of warning the reader about the importance of the entire text. With this alteration to the original text the Two Ways materials were adapted for use as instruction for those persons who wanted to join the Christian community, most likely at the time of preparation for baptism.

The text of chapters 7–15 is not likely to have served this same purpose, that is, as instruction for new Christians. It relates instead to questions concerning appropriate liturgy and church structure. Such issues were the concern of community leaders, not of new members. Here one finds directions for conducting a baptism, the correct timing for fasts, prayers that should be spoken when the community assembles for the sharing of food (perhaps at the **eucharist** or Lord's supper), tests for distinguishing true from false prophets, the appropriate way to receive travelers, the suitable wages

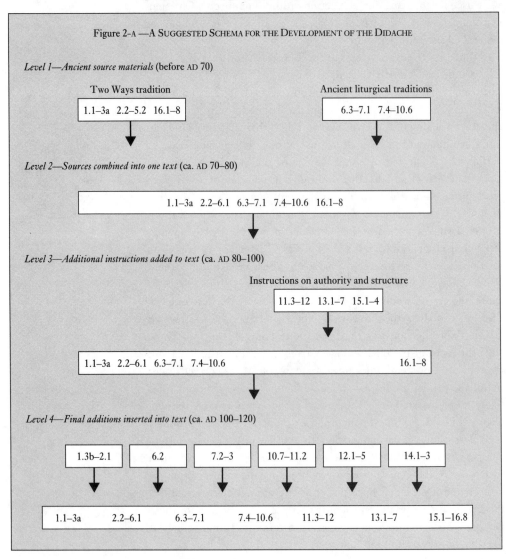

Figure 2-A —A SUGGESTED SCHEMA FOR THE DEVELOPMENT OF THE DIDACHE

Level 1—Ancient source materials (before AD 70)

Two Ways tradition

1.1–3a 2.2–5.2 16.1–8

Ancient liturgical traditions

6.3–7.1 7.4–10.6

Level 2—Sources combined into one text (ca. AD 70–80)

1.1–3a 2.2–6.1 6.3–7.1 7.4–10.6 16.1–8

Level 3—Additional instructions added to text (ca. AD 80–100)

Instructions on authority and structure

11.3–12 13.1–7 15.1–4

1.1–3a 2.2–6.1 6.3–7.1 7.4–10.6   16.1–8

Level 4—Final additions inserted into text (ca. AD 100–120)

1.3b–2.1 | 6.2 | 7.2–3 | 10.7–11.2 | 12.1–5 | 14.1–3

1.1–3a   2.2–6.1   6.3–7.1   7.4–10.6   11.3–12   13.1–7   15.1–16.8

for true prophets, the correct attitude of the gathered community, and the best way to respect community leaders. These materials, many deriving from quite ancient traditions, were preserved as instructions for the leaders of the Didache community. Combined with the Two Ways tradition of chapters 1–6, which by now had been refined specifically for instructing new members, the entire writing probably became a handbook for those who administered the religious and social life of the community.

The Didachist is concerned primarily with the standardization of religious traditions within the community and the relationship of these traditions to correct teaching and community practices. To appreciate how the Didachist directs these concerns, it is important to consider the theological perspective that is at work here. Unfortunately, identifying this perspective with any precision remains tenuous, though certain elements of theology standing behind the use of traditions within the text can be isolated:

2.2.7 What are the primary traits of the text?

(a) Christology. A central part of any discussion of the Didache must focus upon the area of Christology, or the study of the person of Jesus of Nazareth in his role as the Christ. The Didache speaks of Jesus on rare occasion only, and even there with an underdeveloped concept of his role and function as the Christ. It is within the eucharistic prayer of chapter 9 alone that the Didache acknowledges the role of Jesus as the Christ, the servant and child of the Father through whom the knowledge, glory, and power of God are made known. Yet this use of the name of Jesus appears simply as part of the prayer's format, without any specific theological reflection on the part of the Didachist. In other words, there is no mention of Jesus as the Son of God or the significance of that relationship, no understanding of the nature of Jesus as preacher, healer, miracle-worker, or savior. Jesus is called the child of the Father, but this does not distinguish him from the lineage of Israel's great king, David. In the same way, the Didache acknowledges that God is the Father of all persons—with no apparent distinction to be made in the case of Jesus.

The Didache employs the word *Lord* extensively, but the only other mention of the term *Christ* occurs in chapter 12 where the Didache cautions against false prophets who exploit Christ for their own ends. This discrepancy between the frequent use of *Lord* and the limited use of *Christ* may in fact suggest a conscious understanding on the part of the Didachist, who no doubt intends that the term *Lord* serve a double function here. Depending on the theological persuasion of the reader, the term may be perceived as a reference either to God the Father or to Jesus as the Christ.

The Didachist reflects merely a tenuous association between Jesus and the Father that only slightly exceeds the relationship of a prophet with God. One might infer from this that the early Christian community to which the Didache was addressed also had only a vague conception of the role and function of Jesus as the center of Christian theology. For example, the Didache offers no specific reference to Jesus and his relationship to the salvation of humanity. The ideas of sin, repentance, and salvation through the activities of Jesus likewise are absent. Repentance is recognized as necessary for participation in community worship, yet not for salvation.

In these respects, scholars generally acknowledge that the Christology of the Didache is extremely primitive and underdeveloped. In comparison with that of other early Christian writings, the Christology of the Didache is recognized as a *low Christology*.

(b) Regulations for worship. One of the reasons that the Didache is important to students of early church history is that it contains information about how a specific community of Christians after the time of the apostles conducted its liturgy, that is, its celebration of baptism and **eucharist.** The baptismal formula in chapter 6 is the same as that in Matthew 28:19. The details of the instruction show the practicality of the author. Running water (here called *living water*) should be used, though if this is not possible, standing water (presumably rainwater which has been collected into a cistern) is suitable. Cold water also is desirable for baptism, but warm water is acceptable. In each instance the Didachist reflects the typical approach of common Jewish baptisms of the period. No specific reason has been provided as to why a person should be baptized. Modern assumptions that this baptism was meant for a remission or cleansing from sins may not be justified, since baptism for the Didachist may simply have initiated the baptismal candidate into the community.

The thanksgiving prayers of chapters 9–10 likewise have been modeled upon customary Jewish prayers of the period. Most scholars believe that the prayers reflect the blessings of the Jewish meal prayers with a twist of the good news message of early Christianity. If these prayers over the bread and cup do in fact reflect an early approach to the service of the **eucharist,** then it is significant that the meal aspect of the **eucharist** has already been dropped, or at least has become unimportant as a part of the cultic event. Likewise, it is important that the Didache does not preserve any of the traditional words of institution which should be said over the bread and cup according to the apostle Paul in 1 Corinthians 11 and the New Testament Gospels of Matthew, Mark, and Luke. Presumably the Didachist either was unaware of such wording, preferred the thanksgiving prayers in its place, or assumed that the reader would combine the two—thanksgiving prayers and words of institution.

(c) Directions for church structure. Scholars continue to speculate about the nature of the church structure and authority underlying the Didache. According to the text, it appears that the community of the Didachist previously relied on the leadership of wandering prophets, apostles, and teachers. The establishment and leadership of many, if not most, early Christian communities was undertaken by wandering missionaries who proclaimed the gospel and then journeyed on. The apostle Paul was an example of this type of early Christian missionary. Yet even Paul acknowledged the rights and responsibilities of established leaders within certain communities. In the New Testament letter of 1 Timothy, for example, the specific authority of local leaders is identified in a brief description of the office and qualifications for the role of bishop. One discovers that by the end of the first century the concept of a more permanent hierarchy of offices had spread among communities. Indeed, in Didache 15 one finds a reference to the ranks of bishop and deacon, offices which had become a standard part of the community structure of the Didache.

Of primary concern in the Didache is the continued role of wandering apostles and prophets, persons who continued to circulate among the churches during the late first and second centuries. To this one may add the problem of those prophets who attempted to settle within the community. The Didachist advises the community about engaging such persons and cautions about distinguishing false prophets from true ones. All of those who "come in the name of the Lord" should be received, though apostles should not stay more than two days and should ask for nothing more than food and lodging (11.3–6). Prophets should not be examined or tested, though such persons must teach *the truth* and follow what they teach. If such is the case, these persons should receive the portion of food which is due prophets, and they should be permitted to give thanks at community worship as they believe correct.

Those who have studied the text of the Didache have noticed the presence of several distinctive images and ideas. Among the more prominent features, one should be particularly aware of the following:

(a) Two-tiered hierarchy (15.1–2). The Didache speaks of only two ordained offices—bishop and deacon—and not of the three-tiered structure of bishop, presbyter, and deacon that was endorsed by the broader church. It seems remarkable that the community either did not know of the role of presbyter or did not endorse this office. Although this assumption is widely held by scholars, at least two alternatives are possible. In the first case, it is likely that the final form of the Didache itself was constructed as a type of manual for instructing presbyters (not the community at large). Thus the various instructions could be a form of handbook by which presbyters were to conduct their affairs. In the second case, the Didachist may have agreed with the perspective of 1 Clement, which refers to the office of *presbyter-bishop*—a role of leadership that combined the functions of presbyter and bishop.

(b) Trinitarian formula (7.1, 3). The Didache uses the technical formula "in the name of the Father and of the Son and of the Holy Spirit" twice in chapter 7 and in association with the activity of baptism. Although so-called trinitarian language and thought (that is, Father—Son—Holy Spirit) was prevalent throughout early Christianity, it is only at Matthew 28:19 that the phrase is employed in the New Testament. This early use of the formula is associated with the baptism of new converts into the Christian faith both in Matthew and the Didache, and thus suggests some support for the likelihood of a close association between the two texts.

(c) The holy vine of David (9.2). The appearance of these words in the Didache is unique in early Christian literature and cannot be explained with certainty. In the Didache the words have been used as part of the prayer over the cup at the thanksgiving meal. According to the prayer, "the holy vine of David" has been made known through Jesus. This may refer either to the contents of the cup which are drunk for salvation or perhaps to the royal lineage of Jesus who has come as the long-awaited messiah of the church.

(d) Broken bread (9.4). The Greek word translated here as *broken bread* refers in the New Testament Gospels to the pieces of bread that remained after Jesus fed the multitudes. Only in the

Didache does the term become associated with a thanksgiving meal. The Didachist offers the image of bread as a metaphor for the church. For the Didachist, just as bread is formed from grains which have been scattered, grown, harvested, and baked into a loaf, so too the church, which was previously scattered over the earth, may be gathered into the kingdom of God. This passage reflects the desire of the Didachist for the ultimate consummation of the world under the rule of God, a theme occurring elsewhere only in chapter 16.

(e) A worldly mystery of the church (11.11). The Didachist insists that true prophets who "do a worldly mystery of the church," yet do not instruct others to do so, should not be judged by the community. The phrase is unique in early Christian literature and is difficult to understand. It is possible that the phrase is an oblique reference to the celibacy of a prophet, who is to live in a manner reflecting the relationship between Christ and the church. More likely, however, the phrase depicts some early Christian sacrament as the expression of the presence of God within the church, or perhaps refers to some secret of the Christian religion not intended for outsiders.

The Didache is firmly grounded in the Old Testament. The Two Ways tradition already established in Deuteronomy 30 and Jeremiah 6 became the framework for Didache 1–6. In addition, one finds within this framework the use of the **decalogue** in chapters 2–3. Here, as elsewhere in the literature of the period, one discovers the appearance of only five prohibitions—laws against murder, adultery, theft, covetousness, and false witness. The listing of the five functioned as a reference to the validity of all the Ten Commandments. This approach to the **decalogue** typified late Jewish and early Christian literature. In chapter 3 the traditional style of ancient Jewish wisdom literature is employed, a style clearly displayed in the Old Testament text of Proverbs 1–10. The Didachist addresses the reader as *my child* in order to convey the authority of wisdom's teaching and the need to respect and follow the advice that is given.

Occurring throughout the Didache are parallels to the Hebrew Scriptures; presumably these derive from that source. It is clear to see from Figure 2–B that the Didachist draws from numerous writings within the Old Testament. It is equally obvious that the vast majority of these usages fall within the Two Ways tradition. Of course, much of this scripture may already have been present within

2.2.9 How does the text relate to scripture?

Figure 2-B — THE DIDACHE'S PARALLELS WITH THE HEBREW SCRIPTURES

The Two Ways tradition

1.1	Deuteronomy 30:15	2.7	Leviticus 19:17–18		
1.2	Deuteronomy 6:5	3.7	Psalm 37:11		
1.3	Leviticus 19:18	4.13	Deuteronomy 4:2; 12:32		
1.6	Sirach 12:1	5.1	Exodus 20:13–16		
2.2–3	Exodus 20:13–16	5.2	Isaiah 1:23		

The community instruction

12.1	Psalm 118:26
14.3	Malachi 1:11, 14

The concluding warnings

16.7	Zechariah 14:5

Figure 2-C — TEXTS IN THE DIDACHE WITH PARALLELS IN MATTHEW

Didache	*Matthew*	*Content*
1.1	7:13b, 14a	There are Two Ways
1.2	22:37, 39; 7:12	Love God; love your neighbor; golden rule
1.3	5:43–48	Love (pray for) your enemies
1.4–5	5:38–42	Do not retaliate against others
1.5c	5:26	Last penny must be paid
2.2–3	5:21–32; 19:18	Ten commandments
2.7	18:15–17	Do not hate
3.2–6	19:18	Ten commandments
3.7	5:3, 5	Meek shall inherit earth
5.1	15:19	List of vices (Way of Death)
6.1	24:4	Do not be led astray
7.1, 3	28:19	Baptismal formula (Father—Son—Holy Spirit)
8.1	6:16–18	Fasts and hypocrites
8.2a	6:5	Prayer and hypocrites
8.2b	6:9–13	Lord's prayer
9.5	7:6	Do not give holy things to dogs
10.5	24:31	Elect gathered from four winds
10.6	21:9, 15	Hosanna to Son (God) of David
11.3–4	10:40–41	Welcome apostles and prophets
11.7	12:31	Unforgivable sin
11.8	7:15	Distinguish false prophets
12.1	21:9	Receive in name of Lord
13.1	10:10	Prophet is worthy of food
14.2	5:22–24	Reconciliation
15.3	5:22–24; 18:15–17	Discipline and correction
15.4	6:1–18	Prayer, alms, actions
16.1	24:42–44; 25:13	Watch out; be ready; the hour comes
16.3–5	24:10–13, 22–24	Last days
16.6	24:30–31	Signs of truth
16.7	25:31	Holy ones
16.8	24:30; 26:64	Coming of the Lord

some Two Ways source used by the Didachist as the basis for Didache 1–6. Nevertheless, the use and theology of these scriptural texts accord with the author's intentions.

Modern scholars remain undecided about the complicated relationship between the Didache and the New Testament. First, was the Didachist aware of any written gospel, such as those in the New Testament? The Didachist refers to *the gospel* three times: "as the Lord commanded in his gospel" (8.2); "as you find in the gospel" (15.3); and "as you find in the gospel of our Lord" (15.4). It is uncertain, however, whether these references refer to a specific gospel text or to the general message and teachings of Jesus. In addition to explicit references to the gospel, numerous texts appear to reflect the teachings of Jesus but in a slightly different form from that in parallel New Testament materials. It is entirely possible that the Didachist knew of the teachings of Jesus, though not necessarily in the form they ultimately took in the New Testament. The tradition reflected by the Didachist could have been available in a written form, but it is more likely to have come to the author through some oral collection of sayings.

Certain portions of the Didache share an affinity with the theology and language of the Gospel of John and the letters of Paul. But a comparison of the Didache with the entire collection of New Testament writings reveals a significantly high degree of affinity between the Didache and the Gospel of Matthew. Did the Didachist use the Gospel of Matthew directly or, perhaps, a source also employed by the author of Matthew? Scholars continue to debate this issue. The more likely scenario is that the two authors shared the same or a similar source.

2.3 CONTENTS

Outline of the Materials

Summary of the Argument

There are two great paths—one leads to life and the other to death. The first path requires that a person love both God and neighbor. To this end one must endure personal abuse, keep from all evil ways, and follow the commandments of God found in the law and wisdom of Judaism. Small sins lead to greater sins, so seek the support and advice of righteous persons. Treat all persons with the proper respect, maintain a proper household, and keep God's ways. The second path is full of evil actions and thoughts, all of which are counter to the way of life. The believer must not be led astray, but must act appropriately as far as it is possible.

There is also a correct way to conduct one's life of faith and practices. Eat only those foods which are pure to God, baptize in cold running water whenever possible, fast on the appropriate days, and pray with an appropriate prayer three times each day. Certain prayers are suitable when the community gathers to celebrate its relationship with God; other prayers invoke the memory of Jesus. Prayer also seeks the gathering of the church universal and gives thanks for the glory of God. The believer must not be led astray!

Apostles and prophets must be received, though with care. Some may stay; some must go. True prophets deserve a rightful share in the community and must be permitted to conduct liturgies according to their own prophetic wisdom. All quarrels must be put aside when the community gathers for worship. So too, bishops and deacons should be honored, and all disputes must be settled appropriately and in a peaceful way.

The believer must not be led astray! Indeed, the last days will come when the Lord will return in accordance with the signs of scripture.

2.4   RELATED LITERATURE

Barnard, L. W. "The Dead Sea Scrolls, Barnabas, the *Didache* and the Later History of the 'Two Ways.'" In *Studies in the Apostolic Fathers and their Background*. Pages 87–107. New York: Schocken, 1966. (BQ1080.B366 1966)

Court, J. M. "The Didache and St. Matthew's Gospel." *Scottish Journal of Theology* 34 (2, 1981), pp. 97–107.

Draper, Jonathan A. "The Jesus Tradition in the Didache." In *Gospel Perspectives 5: The Jesus Tradition Outside the Gospels*. Edited by David Wenham. Pages 269–87. Sheffield: JSOT, 1985. (BS2555.2.G67 1985)

Jefford, Clayton N. *The Sayings of Jesus in the Teaching of the Twelve Apostles*. Supplements to Vigiliae Christianae 11. Leiden: E. J. Brill, 1989. (BS2940.T5.J44 1989)

Johnson, Sherman Elbridge. "A Subsidiary Motive for the Writing of the Didache." In *Munera Studiosa*. Edited by Massey Hamilton Shepherd Jr. and Sherman Elbridge Johnson. Pages 107–22. Cambridge, Mass.: Episcopal Theological School, 1946. (BS413.M8 1946)

Kraft, Robert A. *Barnabas and the Didache*. The Apostolic Fathers 3. New York: Thomas Nelson & Sons, 1965. (BQ1080.A4 1964)

Milavec, Aaron. "The Pastoral Genius of the Didache: An Analytical Translation and Commentary." In *Religious Writings and Religious Systems* 2. Edited by Jacob Neusner. Pages 89–125. Atlanta: Scholars, 1989. (BL71.R45 1989)

Robinson, J. A. *Barnabas, Hermas and the Didache*. London: S.P.C.K.; New York: Macmillan, 1920. (BQ172.R6 1920)

Vööbus, Arthur. *Liturgical Traditions in the Didache*. Papers of the Estonian Theological Society in Exile 16. Stockholm: E.T.S.E., 1968. (BS2940.T5.V58 1968)

Vokes, F. E. *The Riddle of the Didache: Fact or Fiction, Heresy or Catholicism*. London: S.P.C.K.; New York: Macmillan, 1938. (BQ1302.V6 1938)

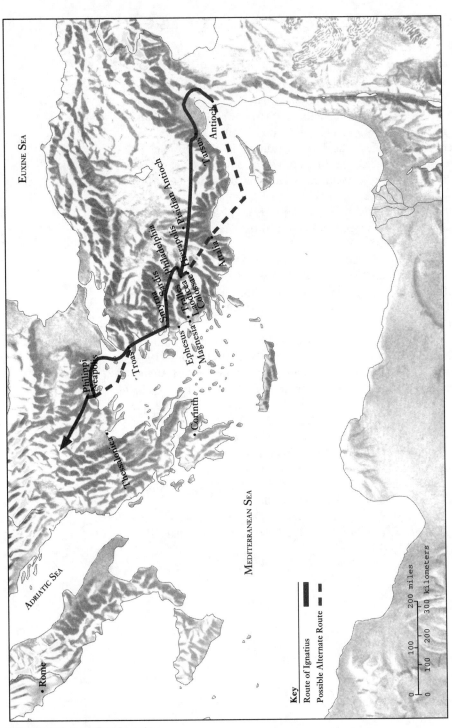

EUXINE SEA

Antioch

Tarsus

Pisidian Antioch

Philadelphia

Sardis

Hierapolis

Smyrna

Attalia

Trallas

Laodicea

Colossae

Ephesus

Magnesia

Troas

Philippi

Neapolis

Corinth

Thessalonica

MEDITERRANEAN SEA

ADRIATIC SEA

Rome

THE ROUTE OF IGNATIUS

Key
Route of Ignatius
Possible Alternate Route

0   100   200 miles
0   100   200   300 kilometers

3 The Letters of Ignatius

3.1.1   Manuscript tradition—three versions with numerous ex-
        amples in Greek, Latin, Syriac, Armenian, Coptic, and
        Arabic
3.1.2   Literary form—early Christian letters or epistles
3.1.3   Authorship—Ignatius (also called Theophorus), second
        bishop of Antioch in Syria
3.1.4   Date—AD 98–117, reign of the emperor Trajan (probably
        around AD 105–110)
3.1.5   Setting—en route from Antioch to Rome (four letters
        from Smyrna, three letters from Troas)
3.1.6   Purpose—to support the development of individual Chris-
        tian communities
3.1.7   Primary elements—false doctrines; Judaizers; church lead-
        ership; creeds; martyrdom
3.1.8   Special images—baptism of Jesus; branches of cross;
        eucharist as flesh; harmony of unity; Onesimus; the divine
        hierarchy
3.1.9   Relationship to scripture—primary focus upon Paul and
        Gospel of Matthew; secondary focus upon themes of John
        and early church teaching; limited use of Old Testament

Of the numerous copies of the letters of Ignatius in existence today, some are more important than others. Yet the history of the preservation of Ignatius's writings indicates that the texts have been valued within the history of Christianity since their composition. It is perhaps of more importance for our present purposes to distinguish among the different groups or versions (often referred to as *recensions*) of manuscripts containing copies of the letters. Since around the

3.2.1 Where did we get our text?

fourth century, the letters of Ignatius have been assembled into three different versions. For lack of a better designation, these versions traditionally are distinguished as the short, middle, and long recensions.

(a) A majority of scholars support the authenticity of the middle recension, which contains letters addressed to the churches at Ephesus, Magnesia, Tralles, Rome, Philadelphia, Smyrna, and the bishop Polycarp (at Smyrna). This collection of texts is preserved in a single Greek manuscript of the eleventh century (Codex Mediceo-Laurentianus 57, 7), a second Greek papyrus text of which only fragments remain, two Latin manuscripts, three sets of Syriac fragments, an Armenian and Arabic extraction of the Syriac form, and two manuscripts in Coptic. It is this middle recension which seems to have been known by the ancient church historian **Eusebius of Caesarea** (*Ecclesiastical History* 3.36).

(b) The short recension is also preserved in Syriac and includes abbreviated forms of the letters to Polycarp, Ephesus, and Rome. The letter to the Romans in this version incorporates a short segment from the letter to Tralles. Although some scholars have argued for the authenticity of this short recension, it seems probable that this version was extracted from a longer collection. There is some reason to think that this abbreviated form of the letters was designed for use among the early monasteries of the medieval period.

(c) The long recension is preserved in several Greek and Latin versions and contains the letters appearing in the middle recension, together with six additional letters: two associated with Mary of Cassobola, and one each to Tarsus (the home of Paul), Antioch, Philippi, and the bishop Heros (the successor of Ignatius at Antioch). Ancient manuscript evidence suggests that these additional writings became associated with the middle recension in at least its Greek, Latin, Armenian, Syriac, and Coptic forms by the fourth century. The origin of these additional writings is unknown.

3.2.2 What form does the text take?

The writings of Ignatius are all constructed in the form of authentic ancient letters. These texts are quite distinct in their presentation of the thoughts of Ignatius, though they follow a standard format and often raise the same general topics of concern. The reader finds most of the typical sections of ancient letters: an introduction, a section of appreciation and thanks for the reader, the reason for the letter, an extensive body or main message of the author, and concluding greetings. The letter to the church in Rome also contains a partial date for the composition of the text, though elsewhere in his letters Ignatius does not indicate the date of his correspondence. In many respects Ignatius modeled the format of his letters upon that of Paul's writings in the New Testament, though, unlike the letters of Paul, Ignatius's letters do not include an ethical section after the main body to challenge his readers to respond to specific topics. Most ancient letters did not make any distinction between the main body and a secondary ethical section, but chose instead to combine the two segments. Ignatius appears to have followed this general practice.

Figure 3–A — Early Christians Known or Mentioned by Ignatius

Name	Reference	Designation
Alce	*Smyrnaeans* 13.2	Christian of Smyrna
	Polycarp 8.3	
Apollonius	*Magnesians* 2.1	presbyter of Magnesia
Attalus	*Polycarp* 8.2	Christian of Smyrna
Bassus	*Magnesians* 2.1	presbyter of Magnesia
Burrhus	*Ephesians* 2.1	deacon of Ephesus
	Philadelphians 11.2	
	Smyrnaeans 12.1	
Crocus	*Ephesians* 2.1	representative of Ephesus
	Romans 10.1	
Damas	*Magnesians* 2.1	bishop of Magnesia
Daphnus	*Smyrnaeans* 13.2	Christian of Smyrna
Epitropus, wife of	*Polycarp* 8.2	Christian of Smyrna
Euplus	*Ephesians* 2.1	representative of Ephesus
Eutecnus	*Smyrnaeans* 13.2	Christian of Smyrna
Fronto	*Ephesians* 2.1	representative of Ephesus
Onesimus	*Ephesians* 1.3; 2.1; 6.2	bishop of Ephesus (cf. Philemon and Colossians 4:16)
Philo	*Philadelphians* 11.1	deacon of Cilicia (city unknown)
	Smyrnaeans 10.1; 13.1	
Polybius	*Trallians* 1.1	bishop of Tralles
Polycarp	*Ephesians* 21.1	bishop of Smyrna
	Magnesians 15.1	
	Polycarp preface; 7.2; 8.2	
Rheus Agathopous	*Philadelphians* 11.1	deacon from Syria (Antioch?)
	Smyrnaeans 10.1	
Tavia	*Smyrnaeans* 13.2	Christian of Smyrna
Zotion	*Magnesians* 2.1	deacon of Magnesia

Without question, the most interesting of the Ignatian texts in terms of style is the letter to the church in Rome. This writing, which in form is less of a casual letter than most of the Ignatian writings, has been cast into what scholars often call a *royal letter* format. The introductory words of greeting here are much more formal in presentation than are those of the remaining letters. So too, Ignatius never commands the Romans in the way that he does his other audiences. Instead, he only makes requests, which the church in Rome was then free to honor or ignore. Unlike most of the Ignatian letters, this letter does not address any specific individuals within the community of Rome. Instead, the letter is offered to the entire assembly before whom it would have been read aloud. The letter to Rome thus suggests that our author, Ignatius, is writing the text from a position of humility, much as a servant would address a master or as a minor public administrator would write to a superior official. The bishop undoubtedly chose this particular letter style for his letter as a way to elicit an appropriate response from persons in a city with whom he was not personally acquainted.

3.2.3 Who was the author?

Each of the seven letters in our collection is specifically identified with the name of Ignatius. Ignatius was an early Christian whose faith in Christ and devotion to the church are evident from his writings. Each of the letters also designates a second name by which he was recognized—Theophorus, which means *bearer of God*. It is quite likely, however, that this was not actually a part of Ignatius's name. Instead, it was probably a nickname or secondary title ascribed to Ignatius by others, perhaps in response to the successful nature of his ministry. A similar name appears at the beginning of the Gospel of Luke and the book of Acts in the New Testament—Theophilus, which means *lover of God*. Here as well, scholars generally recognize that this is not the personal name of any particular individual but, instead, is a title of endearment offered by the author as a friendly gesture. It is even possible that the term was intended to serve as a general title for whoever read these works.

Ignatius served as bishop for the city of Antioch in Syria at the end of the first century and beginning of the second. The fourth-century historian **Eusebius of Caesarea** listed him as the second bishop of that city. Unfortunately, there is no certainty about who was bishop of Antioch prior to Ignatius; **Eusebius** offers two possibilities in his history of the church, the *Ecclesiastical History*. In one passage **Eusebius** mentions the name of Evodius (3.32), an otherwise unknown figure. Shortly afterwards, **Eusebius** insists that the honor should belong to the apostle Peter (3.36). Many historians claim that Peter was the first bishop of the church in Rome.

From his several letters, we can determine that Ignatius was passionate about his faith, that he was concerned for the correct understanding and use of early Christian doctrines and beliefs, and that he was anxious that the structure of authority within the early church develop according to a certain pattern. Ignatius's intensity in discussing these issues was heightened by the threat of his impending martyrdom as he was escorted by soldiers from the city of Antioch to the capital at Rome in the early second century.

We know virtually nothing else with certainty about Ignatius as a person or as a bishop from outside literary sources. Nonetheless, the situation of ancient Antioch may offer some room for further speculation about the person of Ignatius, since his thought and theology were probably greatly influenced by the history of the city itself. Although Antioch was primarily Greek in its customs and culture, it had supported a large Jewish population from around the third century BC. In order to encourage the growth of this population, the Jews of Antioch were gradually granted political privileges and freedoms—favors which unfortunately led to a violent backlash among the remaining residents of the city by the end of the first century AD. Within this context of continual struggle between Judaism and Christianity, a struggle which was both political and theological in nature, Ignatius emerged as a prominent voice within the Christian community.

3.2.4 When was the text written?

Eusebius of Caesarea (*Ecclesiastical History* 3.33–36) places Ignatius's writings within the reign of the Roman emperor **Trajan** (98–117). Though the history of Rome's response to the rise of Christianity varied from one emperor to the next, **Trajan** believed that those proven to be Christians in court should be punished appropriately. The nature of this "appropriate punishment" typically included torture and execution—the very outcome that Ignatius insisted in his letters would eventually come to him.

Several aspects of Ignatius's thought support the view that his ministry was active around the end of the first and beginning of the second centuries. For example, his theology is continually driven by a concern for the end times, that is, for the life of the Christian as it was lived in the last days before the return of Christ. By the middle of the second century this concern within Christianity, which ap-

pears already in the oldest literature of the New Testament (Paul's first letter to the Thessalonians), had finally lost its urgency within the theology of the church.

A second consideration is associated with the issues with which Ignatius struggled, issues that were typical of early Christianity's rise during the late first century. Ignatius wrestled with the threat of Judaism as a theological influence in light of the church's attempt to break its ties with that religion. The resultant temporary void in leadership structures led to an immediate need to construct a reliable framework of authority within the church. Yet even more important was Ignatius's need to convince individual communities to respect that structure. He undertook this task by appealing to the confessions of faith that were observed by the early church. These confessions, or **creeds**, typically acknowledged an understanding of the role of Jesus Christ for salvation which Ignatius believed should serve as the basis of belief throughout all Christian communities and which helped to define his own authority in the role of bishop.

Such elements as these do not date the work of Ignatius with any specificity, yet they do suggest that the bishop was active within the early church as it began to form the policies that directed its development as a religious institution. The scholarly consensus follows the suggestion of **Eusebius** and assigns the letters and death of Ignatius to the reign of **Trajan**, probably even to the middle of that reign—the years 105–110.

3.2.5 In what setting was the text written?

We do not have any Ignatian letters or documents from the time of his work in Antioch. Yet it is clear that his role as bishop within the city eventually led to his arrest by Roman authorities. Some scholars suggest that his arrest resulted from some public actions or comments which he offered by virtue of his authority as bishop. It is more likely, however, that he was arrested because he was a prominent and highly visible leader of a religion—Christianity—which had lost its legal right to exist when its followers were forced out of the Jewish synagogues.

Our information about the situation of Ignatius derives exclusively from the months following his arrest. All the letters were written while Ignatius was in transit to Rome for his trial and execution, an event about which there is no historical record. The traveler from Antioch to Rome had an option of two routes. The first route ran across the western Mediterranean Sea around the island of

Cyprus and thereafter along the southern seacoast of ancient Anatolia (modern Turkey). The other course proceeded entirely across land through the higher, inland hill country. Both routes eventually entered Greece near the ancient city of Troas. Most scholars suggest that Ignatius traveled along the northern route in his journey toward Rome, for the following reasons:

(a) The letters of Ignatius were written from two cities along Ignatius's route—Smyrna and Troas. Of the four texts from Smyrna, three (in addition to the letter to Rome) were sent to cities along the southern route—Tralles, Magnesia, and Ephesus. Each text acknowledges the presence of an envoy sent to Ignatius by the community in question. The presence of these contacts leads most scholars to conclude that these communities sent representatives to the bishop primarily because he had been unable to travel to their cities in person.

(b) Three more letters were written in Troas and were directed to audiences already visited by Ignatius: the churches at Philadelphia and Smyrna, as well as the bishop of Smyrna, Polycarp. Each letter is careful to note the news of peace which has come from Antioch since the departure of Ignatius, a peace about which Ignatius would have been unaware, and about which he was greatly distressed, when he had visited previously with these communities. Logically, it seems that Ignatius must have traveled along the northern route through Philadelphia and Smyrna.

As additional information, the letter of Polycarp to the Philippians traces the journey of Ignatius as far as Neapolis and Philippi in Macedonia (northern Greece); after this the record of his journey has been lost. The words and tone of Ignatius indicate that he was under the pressure of an impending martyrdom, a pressure which undoubtedly shaped his thoughts and perspectives during the course of his writing. History does not record Ignatius's arrival in Rome or provide actual literary evidence for his trial and death there. Historians presume that the bishop did in fact suffer the martyrdom that he had anticipated in his writings.

The purpose for the composition of the Ignatian letters is largely explained by their contents. The primary traits of these contents are reviewed below but are listed here for the sake of convenience:

(a) to combat the presence of false doctrines among the churches of Anatolia and Greece;

3.2.6 Why was the text written?

(b) to offer encouragement to various communities and individual Christians who were tempted to adopt Jewish practices as a part of their faith or to return to the traditions of Judaism altogether;

(c) to encourage Christian unity under the direction of a three-tiered hierarchy of authority, with the bishop guiding each community;

(d) to endorse certain creeds or confessions of Christian belief as a foundation of faith among the churches.

Many of the letters were inspired by the visit of individual bishops who came to consult with Ignatius as he traveled from Antioch to Rome. At the same time, it is obvious that the personal circumstances of Ignatius himself contributed to the letters' origin. For example, at the conclusion of the letters to the Philadelphians and to the bishop Polycarp, Ignatius indicates a desire to assure his readers concerning some information he has received about the newfound peace within his own community in Antioch. He requests that his readers send representatives to Antioch to encourage this peaceful situation because he himself was unable to make this trip.

Perhaps the letter to the church at Rome reveals the most obvious motivation for the composition of any of Ignatius's writings. The tone of this text is altogether different from the remaining letters. No longer is the bishop concerned for issues of false doctrine, Judaism, and church structure. Instead, he appeals to the church of Rome to permit him to suffer a martyr's death—worthy of the Lord—upon his arrival. This letter repeatedly portrays Ignatius as a humble, unworthy servant who envisions himself as serving Christ better through his death than through his life. Scholars continually focus upon this image of Ignatius—the supreme martyr for the Christian faith. It is this image that history has chosen to attach to our author.

Unfortunately, all the writings of Ignatius come from his forced journey to Rome instead of from the period of his service as bishop of Antioch. From what we do have, however, we find a man whose image of himself as a prisoner of the state is much like the apostle Paul in the New Testament. The letters during his journey are directed toward the benefit of the development of individual Christian churches. In only a single writing does he appeal his own case to the community in Rome, and even though he had never visited the city, he could still imagine dying there.

Numerous concerns are addressed throughout the letters of Ignatius, but scholars typically focus upon four primary motifs:

(a) False doctrines. A constant theme is the threat of teachers of false doctrines within the churches. These doctrines generally represent perspectives among the Christians of the late first century that were neither shared nor endorsed by Ignatius. Often these doctrines are called *heresies* by modern scholars, but this label is correct only in the sense that such beliefs ultimately were not accepted by later orthodox Christianity. It is preferable to say that such views became a focus of debate within the early church, and as Ignatius himself claimed, they often led to divisions. The identity of the false teachers, as well as their teachings, is not always clear to the modern reader. Ignatius simply does not provide enough information. Some clues are available, however.

Ignatius occasionally refers to false doctrines as "strange food" or "evil teachings," though the exact nature of his concerns receives little description in these instances. While some scholars believe that Ignatius has several different forms of teaching in mind here, most argue that the bishop's primary concern was to combat the threat of **docetism,** or the belief that Jesus of Nazareth was not truly a human who suffered and died but instead merely assumed the appearance of humanity. Ignatius affords some evidence for this view in his responses to the threat of false doctrines. After warning against the doctrines, he often responds with his own confession of faith in the humanity of Jesus—that Jesus was truly human, having been born of a woman, then having died and received the resurrection of the body. From his consistent, though brief, imagery of the false doctrine he opposes, it is perhaps best to assume that the ongoing threat of **docetism** among the various theologies of early Christianity was the bishop's primary concern throughout his letters.

(b) Judaizers. The separation of the church from Judaism and Jewish traditions receives considerable attention throughout the New Testament. In the letters of Paul (ca. AD 50–64), the apostle often denounces those Christians who insisted that true faith must include a consideration for Jewish traditions and teachings. Scholars refer to those who taught such ideas as *Judaizers*. In some instances these were Jewish converts to Christianity who were determined to remain faithful to their own heritage. In other cases they were

3.2.7 What are the primary traits of the text?

non-Jews who saw little distinction between the customs of Judaism and the teachings of the new Christian faith.

By the end of the first century, within only a few decades of the beginnings of Christianity, Judaism attempted to remove Christians from its midst while Christianity groped to define itself apart from its mother religion, Judaism. This often led to a confusion of structure and doctrine within the fledgling church and forced Christians to define their faith and mission apart from the history and concerns of Judaism. As a result, fear arose that the church would relapse into the religion from which it had only recently departed.

Throughout his letters Ignatius defends Christianity against those insisting that true faith must include at least some devotion to Jewish traditions. At the same time, he is concerned that the church not retreat entirely from the safety of Judaism, which, unlike Christianity, was a legal religion within the Roman Empire. Ignatius offers his principle warnings against the influence of Judaism in *Magnesians* 8–10 and in *Philadelphians* 6. Presumably, it was within the geographical regions of Magnesia and Philadelphia that he had perceived the threat of Judaism to be at its greatest.

(c) Church leadership. Throughout his letters Ignatius reflects an urgent concern to establish a structure of church leadership with three primary levels—bishop, presbyter, and deacon. In this configuration there is a special emphasis on the singular authority of the bishop over all other church positions. Such a structure feels comfortable to many modern Christians, since some version of this pattern continues to exist in most contemporary churches. As a result, many scholars have argued that the views of Ignatius represent that form of church structure which already was dominant at the end of the first century. It is much more likely, however, that the fervent emphasis of Ignatius on this hierarchy of offices resulted from his desire to establish such a structure among the numerous, competing forms of church order that existed throughout Syria, Anatolia, and Greece. Furthermore, while historians have traditionally assumed that Ignatius argued for this hierarchy because he was familiar with it in his home church of Antioch, the opposite situation may in fact have been true. This is to say that he may have felt the need to preach boldly for a threefold hierarchy of offices, because he perceived that this alone was the way to support a system that was not universally accepted among the churches.

Ignatius's dominant concern regarding church hierarchy centers on the need for church unity under a single authority—the

bishop. Consistently throughout the Ignatian letters it is the bishop who has been offered as the center of community authority. As one reads through the letters it is obvious that each work was written either in response to a recent visit by a bishop or in part as a way to show support for a local bishop. The final letter in the collection was even written *to* a bishop—Polycarp of Smyrna. The single exception to this rule occurs with the letter to Rome, where no reference is ever made to the local bishop. There are at least three possible reasons for this omission: (1) Ignatius was so consumed with his main argument that he forgot to mention the bishop; (2) the authority of the bishop in Rome was so secure that Ignatius felt no particular need to comment on the issue; (3) the system of authority in the early Roman church did not include the office of bishop as a central figure.

(d) Creeds. The element that most uniquely characterizes Ignatius among the writings of the apostolic fathers is his consistent use of early Christian creeds or confessions of faith. Ignatius typically offers these confessions either as the rationale behind his numerous theological arguments or as an expression of unity with what he regards as fundamental elements of the Christian faith. Ignatius surpasses every author of New Testament literature in his use of creeds.

The Ignatian creeds primarily emphasize the humanity of Jesus. For example, in *Magnesians* 11 Ignatius offers his belief in Jesus' "birth and suffering and resurrection in the time of Pontius Pilate" as a standard for measuring whatever vain doctrines might challenge the faith of the community. In *Trallians* 9 he again insists that valid faith must acknowledge that Jesus "was of the people of David, from Mary, truly born, ate and drank, was truly persecuted by Pontius Pilate, crucified and died . . . and raised from the dead. . . . " The presence of such creeds indicates that Ignatius values an understanding of faith that includes established formulas for personal confession. In addition, he obviously understands such confessions to be the foundation of a broader church faith, as well as his primary means of influencing the development of neighboring Christian communities.

(f) Martyrdom. The letters of Ignatius show a unique focus on the role and function of martyrdom within the faith of the early church. Whereas Acts 6–8 in the New Testament recounts the death of the deacon Stephen in Jerusalem as the first Christian martyr, subsequent tradition focused on the figure of Ignatius as an exemplar of true faith and religious conviction under the threat of death. Throughout his writings Ignatius refers to his chains of bondage and to the nature of his impending demise in Rome. Yet his greatest reflections upon the significance of martyrdom for faith appear in a single writing—his letter to the church at Rome. The essence of his argument here is that martyrdom allows the Christian to attain unity with God (2.1–2); anyone who is a slave in Christ is free through the resurrection of Jesus (4.3), and earthly kingdoms and desires hold no value for true faith in Christ (6.1–8.1). Perhaps no more vibrant feature of Ignatius's writings exists than his graphic language in *Romans* 4, where he anticipates his death by wild beasts during the games at Rome.

Figure 3-B — EARLY CREEDS USED BY IGNATIUS	
Ephesians 7.2	There is one physician, both flesh and spirit, born and unborn, God in humanity, true life in death, both of Mary and God, subject to suffering yet incapable of suffering, Jesus Christ our Lord.
Ephesians 18.2	For our God, Jesus the Christ, was conceived by Mary in accordance with God's plan, from the seed of David and the Holy Spirit, was born and endured baptism in order to purify the water.
Magnesians 11.1	Be convinced of the birth, passion, and resurrection which occurred in the time of Pontius Pilate's rule. . . .
Trallians 9.1–2	Jesus Christ was from the line of David, of Mary, was truly born, both ate and drank, was truly persecuted under Pontius Pilate, truly crucified and died . . . was truly raised from the dead. . . .
Smyrnaeans 1.1–2	Jesus Christ . . . was truly from the line of David in flesh, Son of God by God's will and power, was truly born of a virgin, baptized by John . . . was truly nailed up under Pontius Pilate and Herod the Tetrarch. . . .

3.2.8 What special images appear?

Ignatius raises numerous themes that were unique within the early Christian tradition, or that now are commonly associated with his unique version of faith in Christ. Several of these elements merit consideration here:

(a) Baptism of Jesus. Ignatius makes a unique observation in the history of Christian doctrine in his claim that the purpose of the baptism of Jesus was "to purify the water" (*Ephesians* 18.2). This observation is offered in order to explain why baptism is an acceptable avenue toward salvation for those who wish to follow Christ.

Undoubtedly, however, it is also a means by which to understand why Jesus, as the messiah of God, was in need of baptism at all. He did not *need* purification but, instead, *submitted* to baptism for the benefit of others. There is no comparable explanation for the baptism of Jesus of Nazareth in the New Testament.

(b) Christians as branches of the cross. In his attack upon heresies, Ignatius notes that such ideas have not been planted by God and thus share no part in a valid interpretation of the death of Jesus. True Christians, however, are as branches of the cross that bear true and incorruptible fruit (*Trallians* 11.1–2). The idea that false teachers bear no fruit for the reign of God is common throughout early Christian literature. Ignatius's vision of a cross with branches, however, clearly associates the symbolism of a productive tree with that of the saving act of Jesus' death upon the cross. This became a vivid sign of unification around which early Christians could shape their theology.

(c) **Eucharist** as the flesh of Jesus. For Ignatius, the correct practice of the **eucharist** is a marker for the unity of the true church. Ignatius has a specific concern that the bread of the **eucharist** be recognized as the actual flesh of Jesus (*Smyrnaeans* 7.1) and that there be only one form of the **eucharist** (*Philadelphians* 4). This concept persisted in certain later Christian traditions which supported the dogma of **transubstantiation,** the belief that Christ is present in the substance of the bread and wine at the **eucharist.** In his concern for the special nature of sacred Christian rituals, Ignatius further insists that no baptism or "agape (meal)," read by many scholars as a reference to the **eucharist,** is valid unless it is directed by the bishop or by some agent of the bishop (*Smyrnaeans* 8).

(d) Harmony of unity. In *Ephesians* 4 and *Romans* 2.2 Ignatius offers the image of the harp and its strings as a metaphor for Christian unity under the authority of the bishop and his presbyters. He urges all members of the church to join in the choir of these unified voices in order to facilitate community harmony as a single voice through Jesus Christ. This imagery perhaps reflects the ancient and widely recognized concept of the *music of the spheres,* the harmonious interaction of those angelic beings who guide the planets and stars along their courses through the skies. For Ignatius, the unified voices of Christian confession are an earthly reflection of that reality as it exists in the world of God.

(e) Onesimus. Scholars have speculated that the Onesimus who is mentioned as the bishop of Ephesus in *Ephesians* 1.3 was in fact the same slave about whom the apostle Paul wrote in his letter to Philemon in the New Testament. While this association suggested some historical connections for the historians of the early church, there is no way to confirm that the references are to be associated with the same person.

(f) The divine hierarchy. As mentioned above, Ignatius was especially concerned that the numerous churches of the Roman Empire recognize the legitimate structure of a threefold hierarchy of authority—bishops, presbyters, deacons. In his efforts to secure some justification for this position, he equates these offices with the imagery of divine authority found in the early Christian tradition. Thus, in *Magnesians* 6 and *Trallians* 3 Ignatius equates the place of the bishop with that of God, the presbyters with the council of the apostles, and the deacons with Jesus Christ. The order of rank for these offices in the early church often is depicted by scholars as bishop—deacon—presbyter because of the rank of authority suggested by the imagery of God the Father—Jesus the Son—twelve apostles. The function and status of these offices, however, is not clear, nor was it so generally acknowledged in a uniform way among the early churches. The presence of presbyter–bishops (a mixed office) seems evident in some communities. It is not certain, however, that Ignatius intended for the presbyters to represent the apostles whom Jesus of Nazareth had chosen to assist him in his ministry. Instead, Ignatius may perhaps have wished to convey the idea that the presbyters were to serve in the same role as the heavenly creatures who formed a divine council of assistance around the heavenly throne of God. In either case it is obvious that Ignatius sought to structure church authority according to his perception of divine authority.

3.2.9 How does the text relate to scripture?

The letters of Ignatius make only a limited use of the Old Testament, with references at *Ephesians* 5.3, *Magnesians* 12, and *Trallians* 8.2. In the first two instances he uses the introductory words "it is written" to indicate that the source of his authority is scripture. *Trallians* contains a vague reference to the book of Isaiah that Ignatius probably inserted from memory. Elsewhere, he includes other scattered allusions to the Old Testament scriptures, but these receive only minor attention.

Since the faith of early Christian theologians was generally conceived and constructed upon the testimony of the Old Testament

authors, it probably would be wrong to assert that Ignatius did not
have any real concern for the scripture of his age. He probably drew
from Old Testament texts that he heard in the worship of the
Christian community at Antioch instead of from texts that reminded
him of the traditions of Judaism. Ignatius seems to select scripture
more on the basis of casual practice and memory than from intensive
study. The Old Testament holds no central place for Ignatius. Instead, he uses its texts simply to support his understanding of
correct Christian beliefs and creeds.

Ignatius's use of New Testament sources has generated much
scholarly discussion. Scholars observe that his writings reveal reflections of theology from the Gospel of John. Parallels to John are
detected in Ignatian phrases such as "bread of God," "seed of
David," "living water," and "Jesus as the door to the Father." The
scattered nature of these phrases suggests that Ignatius may have
been aware of several Johannine themes, but there does *not* seem to
be any specific indication that Ignatius had access to the materials of
the Gospel of John itself.

Because of the presence of numerous parallels and apparent
quotations from Matthew in Ignatius's writings, it seems evident
that Ignatius knew, and probably used, that gospel. An especially
important consideration is the *way* in which he has used the
gospel. The bishop did not tend to use quotations from his source
text, but rather made allusions to Matthean episodes and concepts.
These became the point of contact for his own arguments throughout the letters.

Finally, Ignatius clearly knew Paul's letters and, in fact, shapes
his own correspondence around the model of the apostle. Pauline
ideas and terms are scattered consistently throughout the Ignatian
letters and often serve as the basis for specific argumentation. In the
case of Ignatius's letter to the Ephesians, there is even some reason
to believe that the bishop constructed his work according to the
framework of the New Testament letter to Ephesus. In many respects, it is with both the theology and the works of Paul that we find
the key to Ignatius's own theological speculation and concern for the
Christian life.

In summary, Ignatius seems to have known and used materials
from the Old Testament, the Gospel of Matthew, the letters of Paul,
and other early Christian traditions. Some of these materials are in
the form of creeds, confessions, and hymns. Others reflect early
Christian traditions about the historical Jesus and the risen Christ

that ultimately were subsumed elsewhere into the literature of the New Testament. Ignatius depended greatly upon the work of Paul and the common Christian traditions of the late first century, sources which he has used and manipulated at will. He elaborated freely upon Matthean texts and concepts, though he apparently assumed that his audience knew the text of Matthew as well, and thus he typically has not directly cited the passages in question. He rarely relied upon the Old Testament, undoubtedly because he wanted to avoid any charge that he depended on the traditions of Judaism for his faith.

3.3 CONTENTS

Outline of the Material

(a) LETTER TO THE EPHESIANS
Greeting to church at Ephesus   preface
Thanks for visit of Bishop Onesimus   1.1–3
Request that Burrhus remain to assist   2.1–2
Call for unity in Christ under bishop   3.1–6.1
Warnings against threat of heresies   6.2–10.3
General admonitions in light of end times   11.1–16.2
Explanation of Christ's role in salvation   17.1–20.2
Closing and farewell   21.1–2

(b) LETTER TO THE MAGNESIANS
Greeting to church at Magnesia   preface
Thanks for visit of Bishop Damas and others   1.1–2.1
Explanation of authority of bishop   3.1–4.1
Note on presence of Christ in believers   5.1
Call for unity in Christ under authorities   6.1–7.2
Warnings against threat of Judaism   8.1–10.3
General admonitions   11.1–13.2
Closing and farewell   14.1–15.1

(c) LETTER TO THE TRALLIANS
Greeting to church at Tralles   preface
Thanks for visit of Bishop Polybius   1.1–2
Explanation on authority of leaders   2.1–3.2
Note on authority and knowledge of Ignatius   3.3–5.2
Warnings against threat of docetism   6.1–11.2
Closing and farewell   12.1–13.3

(d) LETTER TO THE ROMANS
Greeting to church at Rome   preface
Request that Romans not intervene   1.1–3.3

Summary of the Argument

(a) Greetings to the Ephesians! You are widely known, and I gladly received your delegation. Live in harmony under your bishop, Onesimus. Assemble together in unity, and avoid outsiders who preach lies. Remain humble and pure in Jesus Christ, for these are the last days. Unlike me, you are free—so resist evil, have faith, and act through love. Avoid false teaching. Come to realize that Jesus came as one of us to abolish death. I hope to write to you again.

(b) Greetings to the Magnesians! I have received your delegation, and I ask that you respect your young bishop, Damas, in Christian faith. God knows the unbelievers, so live in unity with your leaders. Worship together in your faith and avoid the old ways of Judaism. I envy your lives in Jesus Christ—so stand firm in faith. The Ephesians send their greetings.

(c) Greetings to the Trallians! Your bishop, Polybius, sings your praises. Respect him, as well as the presbyters and deacons. Be humble as I am humble, and thus avoid the snares of heresy and false teaching. Keep away from unbelievers who preach that Jesus Christ was not truly human, for they are corrupted. Pray for me. The Smyrnaeans and Ephesians greet you.

(d) Greetings to the Romans! Though I am unworthy, I long to see you. Pray for me. And when I arrive in chains, let me die a martyr's death—eaten by wild beasts! I long for this proof that I am a true disciple of Jesus Christ. Let me follow in the footsteps of the Lord. I no longer take pleasure in life. Pray for the church in Syria.

(e) Greetings to the Philadelphians! Follow your bishop as a shepherd and flee from the wolves of false teaching. Remain unified and practice one **eucharist**. Your prayers support me. Avoid those who preach Judaism. Act as the bishop directs you, and live in the unity of God. I hear that the church in Antioch is now at peace. The church at Troas greets you.

(f) Greetings to the Smyrnaeans! I have seen that your faith is solid. As with me, you see that Jesus Christ suffered as a human and was resurrected in the flesh. Avoid those who preach otherwise in their ignorance. There will be a judgment for these unbelievers. Their false actions and disdain for the **eucharist** condemn them. Honor your bishop and follow him closely. Your prayers and faith have supported me. Send someone to the church in Syria to affirm the peace which has come there. The church at Troas greets you. I greet many people there by name.

(g) Greetings to Bishop Polycarp! Continue in your obligations with diligence. Handle disputes with wisdom and in purity—be God's athlete! Conquer those who teach false ideas. Support the widows and slaves in your midst. To the community—heed your bishop and be unified under his guidance. To Polycarp—send someone to the church in Syria to affirm the peace which has come there. Write on my behalf to those churches which I soon will reach. I greet many people there by name.

3.4 RELATED LITERATURE

Barnard, L. W. "The Background of St. Ignatius of Antioch." *Vigiliae Christianae* 17 (3, 1963), pp. 192–206.

Barrett, C. K. "Jews and Judaizers in the Epistles of Ignatius." In *Jews, Greeks and Christians.* Edited by Robert Hammerton-Kelly and Robin Scroggs. Pages 220–44. Studies in Judaism in Late Antiquity 21. Leiden: E. J. Brill, 1976. (BM176.J43 1976)

Corwin, Virginia. *St. Ignatius and Christianity in Antioch*. Yale Publications in Religion 1. New Haven, Conn.: Yale University Press, 1960. (BQ1526.C6 1960)

Grant, Robert M. *Ignatius of Antioch*. The Apostolic Fathers 4. Camden, N.J.: Thomas Nelson & Sons, 1966. (BQ1080.A4 1964)

_____. "Scripture and Tradition in Ignatius of Antioch." In *After the New Testament*. Pages 37–54. Philadelphia: Fortress, 1967. (BR67.G68 1967)

Jefford, Clayton N. "Ignatius of Antioch and the Rhetoric of Freedom." In *Christian Freedom: Essays by the Faculty of the Saint Meinrad School of Theology*. American University Studies 7/144. Pages 25–39. New York: Peter Lang, 1993. (BT810.2 .C477 1993)

Malina, Bruce J. "The Social World Implied in the Letters of the Christian Bishop–Martyr Named Ignatius of Antioch." In *Society of Biblical Literature 1978 Seminar Papers*. Edited by Paul J. Achtemeier. Volume 2, pages 71–119. Missoula, Mont.: Scholars, 1978. (BS410.S65 1978)

Richardson, Cyril Charles. *The Christianity of Ignatius of Antioch*. New York: Columbia University Press, 1935. (BQ1526.R5 1935)

Rius-Camps, J. *The Four Authentic Letters of Ignatius, the Martyr*. Orientalia Christiana Analecta 213/2. Rome: Pontificium Institutum Orientalium Studiorum, 1980. (BQX5404.O71.V213 1980)

Schoedel, William R. *Ignatius of Antioch: A Commentary on the Letters of Ignatius of Antioch*. Edited by Helmut Koester. Hermeneia. Philadelphia: Fortress, 1985. (BR65.I3.S3 1985)

4 The Letter of Polycarp to the Philippians

4.1.1   Manuscript tradition—one Latin text (complete); nine short Greek texts (chapters 1–9) combined with Barnabas; portions in Eusebius of Caesarea (chapters 9, 13); incomplete Syriac fragments

4.1.2   Literary form—early Christian letter or epistle constructed from two separate letters

4.1.3   Authorship—Polycarp, bishop of Smyrna in Asia Minor (ca. AD 70–ca. 156)

4.1.4   Date—ca. AD 105–110 (chapter 13); ca. AD 120–135 (chapters 1–12, 14)

4.1.5   Setting—Smyrna in Asia Minor

4.1.6   Purpose—to accompany letters of Ignatius (chapter 13); to address theme of righteousness (chapters 1–12, 14)

4.1.7   Primary elements—concern for righteousness; concern for Christian unity

4.1.8   Special images—Christians as worthy citizens; Jesus Christ as eternal priest

4.1.9   Relationship to scripture—broad use of New Testament letters, especially from Paul

4.2 QUESTIONS

4.2.1 Where did we get our text?

It is not easy to reconstruct an accurate text of Polycarp's letter to the church at Philippi from the surviving copies of the work. Much of the original Greek text has been lost over the centuries. Also, it appears that the present text is actually a combination of two separate letters written by the bishop Polycarp on separate occasions—although all of our traditions view these materials as a single letter. The manuscript evidence for the combined text is as follows:

(a) The complete text has been preserved in only one Latin manuscript. Although this text comes from an ancient source, it is primarily a combination of loose paraphrases and thus does not appear to be a particularly faithful witness to the original Greek text. Unfortunately, scholars must rely on this manuscript to reconstruct chapters 10–12 and 14, since these materials have not been preserved in any other literary traditions of the letter.

(b) Portions of the letter have also been preserved in nine Greek manuscripts. The most prominent of these texts is the eleventh-century Codex Vaticanus Graecus 859. It is obvious that these manuscripts all derive from a single literary tradition, since each copy contains chapters 1–9 of Polycarp's letter, followed immediately and without interruption by chapter 5 of Barnabas. Apparently, the entire text was intended to be read as a single writing. In those places where there are inconsistencies among the Greek translations of the manuscripts, scholars usually consult the Latin text since it is based upon an even earlier form of the original Greek letter.

(c) The bishop **Eusebius of Caesarea** preserves a copy of chapters 9 and 13 and thus provides a further addendum to the manuscript tradition of the primary Greek witnesses (*Ecclesiastical History* 3.36.13–15). While **Eusebius,** unlike the Latin tradition, does not contain a reference to the bishop Ignatius at the conclusion of chapter 13, scholars generally assume that the Latin manuscript preserves the more reliable reading here.

(d) Several fragments of chapter 12 exist in the Syriac language, though these are of little value for reconstructing the text.

The text contains two distinct sections. Chapters 1–12 and 14 follow the typical format of the ancient letter style that was illustrated earlier in our discussion of the writings of Ignatius. This format includes an introduction, a section of appreciation and thanks for the reader, the reason for the letter, an extensive body or main message of the author, and concluding greetings.

4.2.2 What form does the text take?

Most scholars think that chapter 13 may have been a separate letter that was incorporated just prior to the concluding greetings of the first letter. Some scholars even argue that chapters 13–14 formed this separate letter. In either case, there are two distinct reasons to think that at least chapter 13 originally was a separate writing from the hand of Polycarp:

(a) In chapter 13 Polycarp's argument turns abruptly to a new topic concerning the bishop Ignatius; the reader has received no preparation for such a shift. True, Polycarp has previously mentioned Ignatius in a short list of martyrs (chapter 9), though he offers no further elaboration here. In chapter 13, however, Polycarp asks the members of the community if they have received any news about the bishop. Most scholars contend that the tone of these two references serves to separate the two statements in time. This would suggest that they were written on different occasions.

(b) The second argument states that, while chapter 3 mentions that Polycarp writes in order to encourage the Philippians with respect to their righteousness, in chapter 13 he offers a different reason for his letter—to forward copies of the Ignatian letters as requested by both Ignatius and the Philippians. It certainly is possible that Polycarp wanted to undertake both tasks in this single document. It is much more likely, however, that the texts of two separate letters to the church at Philippi were combined into a single document, probably as a convenient way to preserve the two texts. The tendency among early church communities to combine short, important letters into larger collections is illustrated by 2 Corinthians and Philippians in the New Testament corpus. Biblical scholars usually view these documents as the compilation of several shorter letters.

Figure 4-A — THE TWO LETTERS OF POLYCARP TO THE PHILIPPIANS?

First Letter (AD 105–110)	*Second Letter (ca. AD 120–135)*
	Chapters 1–3
(Greeting and thanksgiving?)	Greeting and thanksgiving
	Call to righteousness
	Chapters 3–6
	Community instructions
	Chapter 7
	Warning against false teaching
	Chapter 8–10
	Call to perseverance
	Chapter 11
	The apostasy of Valens
	Chapter 12
	Closing blessing and prayers
Chapter 13	
Cover letter for the letters of the bishop Ignatius	
(Chapter 14?)	(Chapter 14?)
Closing and farewell	Closing and farewell

While most scholars accept the hypothesis that two distinct letters were combined into a single text, objections have been raised. The primary objection is that Polycarp's focus upon the bishop Ignatius which appears in chapter 13 occurs in only a single Latin manuscript of poor quality. Indeed, as seen above, **Eusebius** contains no such reference to Ignatius in his version of these same materials. Despite this concern, it is generally agreed that the early church at Philippi had chosen to combine two letters into the single work we now possess.

4.2.3 Who was the author?

The present title of our letter ascribes the authorship of the text to "the saint Polycarp, bishop of Smyrna and holy martyr." While the designations *saint* (or holy) and *martyr* leave no doubt that this is a later ascription, there also is little question that the author is the man Polycarp, the bishop of the Christian community in Smyrna during the early second century.

Polycarp's life is traditionally dated to that span of time linking the final years of the apostles of Jesus to the next generation of early Christians (ca. 70–ca. 156). According to how one reads the Roman calendars of the period, the date of his death has been established as either 23 February 155 or 22 February 156. The Martyrdom of Polycarp (see 9.3) records that the bishop lived to the age of eighty-six; this places his birth around AD 69–70. **Eusebius** wrote (*Ecclesiastical History* 5.20.5–8) that, according to **Irenaeus,** Polycarp was a disciple of John the apostle. Furthermore, John was purported to have appointed Polycarp to be bishop of the community at Smyrna. Because of his long life, Polycarp generally is seen as an important link in the continuity of the early church in the region of Asia Minor. **Irenaeus** also states that Polycarp wrote additional letters to other communities, although our current letter is Polycarp's only surviving writing.

The various details of Polycarp's life are no longer certain. Without question, however, early church historians and theologians considered him to have been a prominent Christian leader. This prominence is perhaps best illustrated by the portrait of Polycarp appearing in the early fifth-century text of *A Life of Polycarp.* Though erroneously attributed to **Pionius,** a third-century presbyter from Smyrna, the *Life* presents a fictional account of the activities of Polycarp in order to glorify the memory of the bishop.

One common piece of tradition about Polycarp involves his encounter with **Anicetus,** an early bishop of Rome, and their discussion about the date of Easter. Bishop **Anicetus** and most of the churches of the western empire celebrated Easter on the Sunday following Passover. Polycarp and the churches of Asia Minor, however, observed Easter according to the Jewish dating of the Passover, on the fourteenth day of the Hebrew month of Nisan, and celebrated it on any day of the week, depending on its date according to the Roman calendar. While history records that the two men did not resolve their differences on this issue, they did agree to maintain their separate practices and managed to part in peace.

4.2.4 When was the text written?

Of the two writings thought to have been combined to form our present letter, the text of chapter 13 is the earlier and was essentially written during the same period of time as the letters of Ignatius (ca. AD 105–110). Scholars generally assume this to be true both because this chapter is concerned with the letters of Ignatius themselves and because of the context in which Ignatius is mentioned. The chapter begins by observing that Ignatius wanted the Philippians to receive a copy of his letters. It ends with a request from the Philippians about any knowledge they might have concerning Ignatius and his companions. The tone of these materials implies that Ignatius had only recently communicated with Polycarp, who probably anticipated the martyrdom of Ignatius. At the same time, Polycarp's question with regard to the situation of Ignatius suggests that he had not yet heard any word about Ignatius's actual death.

The remaining portion of the text, chapters 1–12 and 14, is often dated during the years AD 120–135. The various arguments with respect to these dates assume that Polycarp is referring to the early heretic **Marcion** of Sinope when he alludes to the "firstborn of Satan" in chapter 7. These dates allow both for a development of **Marcion's** theology (which Polycarp presumably opposed) and for the letter's extensive use of New Testament writings. Apart from such limited criteria, however, it is difficult to date the text of Polycarp's letter(s) with any accuracy.

4.2.5 In what setting was the text written?

Although no location is given for the city in which Polycarp's text was written, it can be safely assumed that this work was composed in Smyrna of Asia Minor. This holds true whether one considers that the text was originally only a single letter or was two separate writings which the subsequent literary tradition combined into a single, unified form.

The reasons for this assumption are clear. In the first place, Polycarp enjoyed a long period of leadership as bishop of the community at Smyrna. In this position of authority he would naturally have addressed his letters to other churches from his home city. In addition, the title of our current text, which has been added by the early Christian tradition, associates the materials of the letter with Polycarp's role as bishop of Smyrna.

Neither of these observations can be seen as conclusive proof for identifying Smyrna as the only site of the text, of course. Indeed, many early Christian leaders composed their letters as they traveled around the Mediterranean world, such as the apostle Paul and the bishop Ignatius. Moreover, history records that Polycarp himself journeyed as far away as Rome. Yet the place of Polycarp in early church history reflects the gradual development of specific, community leadership and a unified structure of administration among local churches at the beginning of the second century. Because scholars almost unanimously acknowledge this process of institutionalization within the early church, no serious objection has ever been raised to the city of Smyrna as the setting for any of the materials which appear here.

If we can assume that the text was originally two separate letters, then the purpose for the writing of each of the letters should be readily distinguishable. The earlier letter—the materials preserved in chapter 13—acknowledges that Polycarp had attached this short text to his personal collection of letters from Ignatius, a collection he subsequently sent to the Christian community at Philippi. By all appearances, therefore, this chapter was simply a cover letter to the Ignatian letters. The evidence indicates that both Ignatius and the church at Philippi had requested that these letters be sent.

The broadly stated purpose of the second letter—chapters 1–12 and 14—may be found in chapter 3 of that material. The body of Polycarp's letter begins at chapter 3 with what appears to be a general apology, or explanation, for the writing. Polycarp reveals that he is humbled to write to a community that has already been graced by a letter from the apostle Paul, the text of which has been preserved in the letter of Philippians in the New Testament. Fur-

4.2.6 Why was the text written?

thermore, Polycarp intends to address the Philippians about the theme of righteousness, because they "first invited me" (3.1). He continues to pursue this motif throughout the next eight chapters.

Scholars often have argued that, in addition to the theme of righteousness, Polycarp is motivated by a community scandal centering around either a heretical teaching or a questionable individual:

(a) In chapter 7 Polycarp admonishes the Philippians that "anyone who does not confess that Jesus Christ has come in the flesh is an antichrist" (7.1). It is quite possible that this warning against the threat of **docetism** within the community is not simply a random warning, but a response to an immediate concern facing the Philippians. If this is the case, then Polycarp's reason for writing this letter is driven as much by his concern for heresy as by his need to speak on the theme of righteousness in general.

(b) In chapter 11 Polycarp laments that a former leader among the Philippians—the presbyter Valens—has chosen to neglect his duties within the congregation. Some scholars suggest that this individual had been exiled from the community, perhaps because of a scandal concerning greed or some other abuse of his powers of authority.

While either one of these explanations may be important reasons for the composition of Polycarp's letter, there seems to be no persuasive evidence that these are more than secondary interests. Neither the theme of **docetism** nor of abuse of power figures prominently. Instead, each theme is only briefly discussed later in the text. If either of these had been the primary purpose for the composition of the letter, one might expect a stronger and more direct confrontation with the issues.

It may be best to assume that Polycarp wrote this second letter in response to a request by the Philippians for some general teaching on righteousness. While that request may have been instigated because of some specific concerns about the teachings of **docetism** or abuses of power within the leadership of the community, these are only examples of a larger concern within the church.

4.2.7 What are the primary traits of the text?

Since the text of Polycarp's letter is rather brief, it does not provide a wealth of information either about the bishop and his personal concerns or about those issues which defined his activities while leader of the church in Smyrna. At the same time, however, certain elements characterize the letter as a whole. These elements are as follows:

(a) Concern for righteousness among Christians. The motif of righteousness, which is emphasized as well in the Gospel of Matthew in the New Testament, became a prominent concern as early Christian communities settled into established locations and integrated their lifestyles into local settings. Scholars have noted that the earliest Christians were focused to a large extent upon missionary activity and the spread of their gospel message among the nations of the Mediterranean world. This movement was driven by a deep conviction that history would soon end and that a new kingdom would be established by God for those who were faithful to the gospel message. Evidence of this view is prevalent throughout the scattered **apocalyptic literature** of early Christianity.

Polycarp exemplifies the realization among Christians at the end of the first century that the establishment of such a kingdom either had been postponed or had come into existence only in a spiritual sense. The obvious choice then was to refocus the concerns of the church toward an ethical message that was based upon the individual's love of God and respect toward neighbors. For Polycarp, this dedication was measured by the degree to which Christians sought to be righteous in the eyes of God

The letter of Polycarp focuses primarily upon this theme, presumably at the request of the Philippians (3.1). In this cause, to have love for another person serves to keep the faithful Christian free from all sins (3.3). The structure of the letter is itself focused upon the illustration of this motif of righteousness as it appears in typical Christian living. Righteousness demands appropriate interaction among spouses and among the different levels of church leadership (chapters 4–6); righteousness avoids false teaching and the pursuit of individual gain, which lead to division among Christians (chapters 7 and 11); righteousness insists upon perseverance in the face of persecution, as is modeled by the lives of those who became martyrs for the faith (chapters 8–10). As the bishop observes in 8.2, in all of these ways the believer's pledge for righteousness is fulfilled in the figure of Christ Jesus who took upon himself the sins of the world through his death.

(b) Concern for unity. An underlying focus of Polycarp's message is the need for unity within Christian communities. This concern was emphasized already by Ignatius as he traveled through Asia Minor and Greece toward his impending death at Rome. Presumably, Polycarp here echoes a common concern among early church leaders who found themselves at the beginning of debates and decisions on questions of doctrine and belief, a process that eventually led to a series of church councils which met to decide such issues in subsequent centuries.

In chapter 7 Polycarp confronts the problem of community division in his attack upon the challenge of **docetism**. From the content of the materials we may ascertain that there was a person or group of persons within the community who questioned the humanity of Jesus of Nazareth, as well as the reality of his death upon the cross and his subsequent resurrection as an act of salvation for the world. Polycarp makes it clear that to claim that Jesus was never truly human, but only a divine being who assumed the form of a man, is to maintain the view of an "antichrist," one who is "of the devil," and even to be "the firstborn of the devil." According to **Irenaeus** (*Against Heresies* 3.3.4), it was by the last of these phrases that Polycarp described the second-century heretic **Marcion,** whom many scholars see as a specific object of scorn in this chapter.

Chapter 11 is a combination of the admonition to avoid the love of money and the summons to forgive a fallen presbyter named Valens. Valens presumably was in a position of trust yet abused his responsibilities through his greed. Although Polycarp raises the subject of Valens, he does not wish to focus upon the man himself but upon the need for the Philippians to realize that money can quickly become an idol. The bishop encourages the Philippians to open themselves to the return of Valens so that the community might be whole again. Such actions are more than noble, they are preferable for unity.

4.2.8 What special images appear?

Though Polycarp seems to have been widely known and respected among early Christian leaders and historians, the letter he penned offers few special or imaginative images which can be associated with his thought. The few images that should be observed are as follows:

(a) Worthy citizens of God's community (5.2). With this phrase Polycarp reflects a growing realization within early second-century Christianity that loyalty to the community of Christ may be depicted along the model of loyalty to the secular government. The same idea surfaces in the roughly contemporary writings of 1 Clement, the Shepherd of Hermas, and the Letter of Diognetus, and received extensive development among later church authors—especially the theologian **Augustine** of Hippo. This element of Polycarp's thought indicates that the church had gradually become an established segment of ancient culture and society. Its constituents had valid social and economic responsibilities in the world, and the values which accompanied these obligations could be viewed as legitimate within the structure of the institutional church as well.

(b) Jesus Christ—the eternal priest (12.2). The identification of Jesus of Nazareth with the status of priest is not widely attested in early Christian literature. The single example of note occurs in the book of Hebrews in the New Testament, where Jesus is identified as the "great high priest" of God according to the royal order of the priest Melchizedek, who is known to us from Genesis 14 (see Hebrews 4:14–5:10). Polycarp's primary concern in this section is to assure the Philippians that the resurrected Jesus is in a position to build the faith of the community and mediate on their behalf with God the Father. In the view of traditional Jewish-Christian thought, this was the value of a priest within the religious tradition—a mediator between the divine and the human.

The text is inundated with quotes from the scriptures, though very few of these are from that traditional standard of authority, or **canon,** which was recognized within the early church—the Old Testament. The way in which Polycarp employs the writings of the New Testament, however, has been compared with the way in which the author of Barnabas uses the Old Testament. While Polycarp draws upon a broad variety of texts in order to build his argument, he offers no extensive analysis of any particular passage. It appears from a remark in chapter 12 that Polycarp did not even believe himself to be well-versed in the scriptures. Yet his extensive use of certain New Testament authors indicates both that he was well-acquainted with the literature of faith circulating within the second-century Christian tradition and that he had ample access to a great number of early Christian texts. In evidence among Polycarp's sources are the authentic letters of Paul, the so-called Pastoral Epistles (1–2 Timothy and Titus), 1 Peter, and 1 John. While it is generally accepted that he did not have an understanding of the four Gospels as such, he did make some limited use of the Gospel of Matthew and obviously recognized the authority of that gospel tradition. In addition, Polycarp's letter indicates quite clearly that he

4.2.9 How does the text relate to scripture?

had access to the writing of 1 Clement (see 9.2) and to the letters of Ignatius (see chapter 13), except perhaps for the Ignatian letter to Rome, which circulated under a different literary tradition.

4.3   CONTENTS

Outline of the
Materials

GREETING TO CHURCH AT PHILIPPI   preface
THANKSGIVING   1.1–3
CALL TO SERVE AND TRUST IN GOD   2.1–3
CONCERNING RIGHTEOUSNESS   3.1–12.1
   Praise for the example of Paul   *3.2–3*
   Instructions for the community   *4.1–6.3*
     To the men, their wives, and widows   4.1–3
     To deacons, young men, and virgins   5.1–3
     To presbyters   6.1
     General call to forgiveness and service   6.2–3
   Warning against false teaching   *7.1–2*
   Call to perseverance   *8.1–10.3*
     In imitation of Christ   8.1–2
     In imitation of the martyrs   9.1–2
     Call to steadfast unity   10.1–3
   The apostasy of the presbyter Valens   *11.1–12.1*
CONCLUDING PRAYERS   12.2–3
COVER LETTER FOR THE LETTERS OF IGNATIUS   13.1–2
CLOSING AND FAREWELL   14.1

Summary of the
Argument

Greetings to the Philippians! I rejoice that you help those who will be martyrs for Christ and that you maintain a strong faith. Just as God raises the dead, so too will you receive support for your faithful deeds.

I must speak to you about righteousness—with the apostle Paul as our supreme example. Have no love for money. Let wives be faithful in love and purity; let widows pray in faith. Deacons must be without fault, and so too the young men and virgins. And presbyters must show compassion, since we have no right to ask God for forgiveness if we ourselves do not offer the same to others. There are false teachers among us who claim that Jesus was not truly human but only appeared as such. You, however, must maintain your hope in Christ Jesus, and imitate the endurance which he showed in his suffering. His servants have suffered in righteousness before you. Follow their example.

I grieve to hear that the presbyter Valens has strayed. Avoid all evil yourselves and merit the praise which Paul once offered on your behalf. As for Valens and his wife, be open to their return. Do not be angry.

May God give you strength. Pray for all peoples. I attach the letters of Ignatius which you requested from me. Receive this letter and my greetings through my messenger Crescens.

4.4   RELATED   LITERATURE

Barnard, L. W. "The Problem of St. Polycarp's Epistle to the Philippians." In *Studies in the Apostolic Fathers and their Background.* Pages 31–40. New York: Schocken, 1966. (BQ1080.B366 1966)

Cadoux, C. J. "Polycarp's Two Epistles to the Philippians, by P. N. Harrison." *Journal of Theological Studies* 38 (2, 1937), pp. 267–70.

Carroll, Howard. "Polycarp of Smyrna with Special Reference to Early Christian Martyrdom." Ph.D. dissertation. Duke University, 1946.

Clarke, C. P. S. *St. Ignatius and St. Polycarp.* London: S.P.C.K., 1930. (no reference number)

Gloucester, A. C. "The Epistle of Polycarp to the Philippians." *Church Quarterly* 141 (1, 1945), pp. 1–25.

Harrison, P. N. *Polycarp's Two Epistles to the Philippians.* Cambridge: Cambridge University Press, 1936. (BR65.P62 1936)

Nielsen, Charles M. "Polycarp and Marcion: A Note." *Theological Studies* 47 (2, 1986), pp. 297–99.

Norris, F. W. "Ignatius, Polycarp, and I Clement: Walter Bauer Reconsidered." *Vigiliae Christianae* 30 (1, 1976), pp. 23–44.

Schoedel, William R. *Polycarp, Martyrdom of Polycarp, Fragments of Papias.* Pages 3–49. The Apostolic Fathers 5. New York: Thomas Nelson & Sons, 1965. (BQ1080.A4 1964)

_____. "Polycarp's Witness to Ignatius of Antioch." *Vigiliae Christianae* 41 (1, 1987), pp. 1–10.

5 The Martyrdom of Polycarp

5.1 ANSWERS

5.1.1 Manuscript tradition—seven Greek texts (some complete, some fragmentary); one Latin text; quotation in Eusebius of Caesarea (chapters 1–19); several fragmentary translations of Eusebian text in Syriac, Coptic, and Armenian

5.1.2 Literary form—first instance of Christian martyr acts contained in letter form

5.1.3 Authorship—Christians of Smyrna in Asia Minor (letter form by Evarestus)

5.1.4 Date—AD 155–160 (possibly AD 170–180)

5.1.5 Setting—general Christian persecutions in Smyrna

5.1.6 Purpose—to honor the memory of Polycarp and encourage others who are persecuted

5.1.7 Primary elements—noble death; war between good and evil

5.1.8 Special images—the atheists; prayer of Polycarp; sweet aroma of death; a martyr's birthday; the catholic church

5.1.9 Relationship to scripture—primary focus upon the image of the arrest, trial, and crucifixion of Jesus of Nazareth from the New Testament gospels

5.2 QUESTIONS

5.2.1 Where did we get our text?

Three different categories of texts serve as sources for the Martyrdom of Polycarp. The Martyrdom is found in seven Greek manuscripts, the fourth-century *Ecclesiastical History* of **Eusebius of Caesarea,** and a single Latin manuscript. There are also parts of some brief segments of the Martyrdom in the Syriac, Coptic, and Armenian languages, but these are taken from translations of **Eusebius's** work and thus are not of value as independent sources.

(a) The most important of the three categories of texts is the tradition of the Greek manuscripts, all of which come from the tenth through the thirteenth centuries. The seven manuscripts currently are scattered among various collections throughout Europe and include the well-known **Codex Hierosolymitanus** of Jerusalem, which contains various other writings from the apostolic fathers as well. Six of the manuscripts provide a similar form of the Martyrdom and thus are believed to represent a single textual tradition, or family of texts. While these six texts witness to the tradition which is in general agreement with respect to wording, several of the copies are in poor condition and some exist only in fragments.

In several ways the final manuscript departs significantly from this family of texts. This manuscript is the Moscow Codex (also known as Codex Mosquensis), which was written in the thirteenth century and is located in the Library of the Holy Synod in Moscow. Without question, the most important difference between this **codex** and the remaining texts occurs in the last portion of the final chapter, specifically at 22.2–3. The Moscow Codex offers a more elaborate ending to the Martyrdom. This ending stands as a useful witness to our understanding of the text, since it obviously derives from a tradition independent from the other manuscripts.

(b) The second category of texts appears in the writings of **Eusebius of Caesarea.** In his *Ecclesiastical History* 4.15, which was written around AD 324–325, **Eusebius** records the majority of the Martyrdom, though he seems simply to have paraphrased the text of 2.2–7.3 and has not recorded any material from the end of the text (19.2–22.3). Since these concluding materials serve primarily as a historical witness to the transmission of the text, it is possible that **Eusebius** was unaware of their existence. The omission of materials only serves to emphasize the importance of the ending of the Moscow Codex as a second witness to the conclusion of the text.

(c) Finally, the Latin version of the text dates from the tenth century. While it is valuable to have this independent witness to the Martyrdom in a Latin translation, it does not offer any significant variants upon the text.

The Martyrdom is in many respects the combination of two literary forms. On the one hand, the text is constructed as a letter sent by the church at Smyrna to the church at Philomelium. Philomelium was a small city in the Roman province of Phrygia (middle

5.2.2 What form does the text take?

of modern Turkey) situated about fifteen miles northeast of Pisidian Antioch (not to be confused with the city of Antioch in Syria where Ignatius was bishop). Although sent specifically to the Philomelians, and apparently by their own request (according to 20.1), the letter was also intended for circulation among all of the congregations of the region. As a letter the Martyrdom contains an initial greeting and blessing, a body of material concerning the story of Polycarp's death, and a closing.

The letter form was popular among early Christians, as is attested by the numerous letters of Paul in the New Testament. The authority both of Paul and of his letters had become well established by the second century. Thus the author of the Martyrdom chose this form of communication as a means of asserting his authority and honoring the apostle. Specific elements within the Martyrdom indicate a knowledge of other Christian letters as well. For example, scholars often note that the blessing at the end of the Martyrdom's introduction—"May the mercy, peace and love of God the Father and our Lord Jesus Christ be increased"—is a conscious reflection of Jude 2 in the New Testament. So too, the offer of praise to Jesus Christ which appears at the end of chapter 21 has close parallels to the closing words of 1 Clement (see 65.2).

The Martyrdom is typically recognized as the earliest of the *martyr acts* from the ancient Christian tradition. The theme of martyrdom enters Christian literature through the Jewish martyrs literature of 2 Maccabees 6–7 in the Old Testament **Apocrypha** and through the account of the death of the heroic Stephen in Acts 7 of the New Testament. The presumed martyrdoms of the apostles Peter and Paul in Rome, as well as the anticipated death of Ignatius in that same city, became a common background against which to depict the noble death of Polycarp as a true testimony of faith. Such images gradually became popular events in the mind-set of Christians who faced harassment by nonbelievers. Subsequent literature offers numerous martyrological episodes of famous Christians who died at the hands of persecutors. Within this tradition, the Martyrdom of Polycarp arises as the first instance of this literary form preserved by church history.

5.2.3 Who was the author?

The author of the Martyrdom is never clearly identified at any place throughout the text. A note in 20.2 claims that someone named Evarestus was responsible for the current letter to the Philomelians containing the episode of Polycarp's death. This otherwise unknown person, however, was probably not the author of the original account.

We are told that the author of the Martyrdom was an eyewitness to the death of Polycarp. While there is nothing to support this claim, there likewise is nothing which discredits such an idea. The plural pronoun *we* in 15.1 actually suggests that more than one person may have been responsible for the text. Some scholars believe that these eyewitnesses were early Christians who had themselves escaped martyrdom in Smyrna. Such eyewitnesses may have seen themselves as those who had been preserved through the divine will of God from a fate which was similar to that of Polycarp. In any case, it seems clear that in some way the church of Smyrna that produced our text in its current letter form was the same general community who had witnessed the death of the bishop and recorded its significance for posterity.

Chapter 22 is an addition by a later scribe named Socrates—or Isocrates in the Moscow Codex. Socrates mentions a certain Gaius who had copied the account of Polycarp's death from Irenaeus, the disciple of Polycarp. In 22.3 an additional person named Pionius adds a final note to the document. This Pionius was a presbyter in Smyrna who eventually was martyred himself in the year 250. Previous scholars often observed that this Pionius may have been the same person who later wrote *A Life of Polycarp* since the presbyter has recorded in the Martyrdom that he intended to write a further explanation of a vision that he purportedly received from Polycarp. More recent research indicates, however, that the *Life* was probably composed by a later Christian around the year 400.

There is practically no external evidence for dating the composition of the Martyrdom. Historians have found it much more promising to assign a date to the actual martyrdom of Polycarp himself. Two traditions assist scholars in this effort:

(a) The first tradition appears in chapter 21 of the Martyrdom, which probably has been added to the original text as historical evidence for the transmission of the manuscript. This chapter dates the death of Polycarp specifically to late February, seven days before a great sabbath. Ancient historians marked the years by the reign of important government authorities and religious rulers. So here as well, our author places the martyrdom of Polycarp within the rule of the Proconsul Statius Quadratus, whose proconsulship occurred

5.2.4 When was the text written?

during the years 154–155. Furthermore, chapter 12 refers to Philip the Asiarch, whose reign can be assigned to the sixth decade of the second century. Based upon this information, the date of Polycarp's death is traditionally assigned to 23 February 155, though many recent scholars prefer the later date of 22 February 156.

(b) The second line of consideration follows the witness of **Eusebius,** who places the year of Polycarp's death at 166 (or perhaps 167). This would fall well within the reign of the Roman emperor **Marcus Aurelius,** who ruled during the years 161–180 and permitted the persecution of Christians throughout the empire. Those scholars following **Eusebius's** date often doubt the validity of the references in chapters 12 and 21. In support of this argument, they refer to the appearance of one Quintus, a Phrygian, who is mentioned in chapter 4. The term *Phrygian* is often connected by early historians with the religious sect of **Montanism,** which developed under the teachings of the prophet Montanus around the year 170. According to this view, the reference to a Phrygian—a spurious Christian at best—would postpone the martyrdom of Polycarp to roughly a decade after 155–156.

In either of these cases, scholars assume that the Martyrdom was composed by an actual witness to the death of the bishop Polycarp; this person then composed the original text only a short time after the event. Traditionally, scholars date the text somewhere during the years of 155–160, though the decade of 170–180 during the persecutions of **Aurelius** is certainly possible.

5.2.5 In what setting was the text written?

The contents of the Martyrdom suggest that the work was produced within a context of religious persecution at the hand of government authorities. The fact that the introduction ascribes the letter to the church in Smyrna, together with the certainty that the account portrays the recent death of a bishop of that same city, leaves little question that the original portrayal of the martyrdom was written in or around Smyrna. Since our text concludes with notations by several persons concerned to authenticate the testimony of the original author, it seems reasonable to assume that the account of Polycarp's martyrdom was recorded during the years immediately after the bishop's death.

The latter half of the second century was a time of general intolerance with respect to the growth of Christianity within the Roman Empire. The scattered harassment of Christians by local authorities was widely tolerated and often encouraged. The account of Polycarp's death was recorded as early Christians grew concerned over their legal and religious status within the Roman Empire. The environment of fear and persecution facing these Christians is tempered throughout the text by the elements of hope for the future and reverence for Polycarp's personal faith which were evident within the church at Smyrna.

<hr>

There is no question that the original, historical record of Polycarp's martyrdom was intended to serve both as a means for honoring the memory of a respected bishop and as a form of comforting the faithful in the face of future harassment. Since this account appears to have been rewritten into the form of a letter sent to the church in Philomelium shortly thereafter, we probably should assume that the Christians in that region had themselves come under the threat of persecution. Unlike many of the writings in the apostolic fathers, the text of the Martyrdom does not desire to admonish its readers concerning any particular teaching of the faith, but is concerned instead to demonstrate the true nature of a valid martyrdom—presumably then to serve as a model for encouragement.

5.2.6 Why was the text written?

Figure 5-A — SOME OF THE ACTS OF THE MARTYRS IN EARLY CHRISTIAN LITERATURE

Text	Year	Place of Death
Acts of the Apostles, chapter 7 (New Testament)	35–45	Jerusalem
Martyrdom of Polycarp	155–156	Smyrna
Acts of St. Carpus, Papylus and Agathonice	161–169	Pergamum
Acts of St. Justin and his Companions	165	Rome
Letter of the Churches of Vienne and Lyons to the Churches of Asia and Phrygia	177–178	Lyons
Acts of the Martyrs of Scilli in Africa	180	Numidia
Acts of Apollonius	180–185	Rome
Passion of Perpetua and Felicitas	202	Carthage
Proconsular Acts of St. Cyprian	258	Carthage

The image of the martyr in the early church quickly came to represent the height of true gospel faith. The martyr, through his or her death, was generally believed to offer the ultimate imitation of Jesus of Nazareth's own sacrifice (1.2). Historical records suggest that the story of Polycarp's death soon bolstered other Christians in adversity. His life became a model to be imitated. Curiously, there emerged a band of Christians who deliberately sought martyrdom because they thought that such an end was the true calling of a Christian. The leaders of the church soon strongly discouraged this practice, however. They counseled that if martyrdom must be confronted, then one should not necessarily seek to avoid it—but by the same token, one certainly should not provoke it. In keeping with this teaching, the author of the Martyrdom discourages pursuing martyrdom as inconsistent with the basic teachings of the gospel.

5.2.7 What are the primary traits of the text?

This document does not hold any special interest with respect to the development of early Christian theology. Yet two basic features of the letter should be noted, each of which is focused upon the central image of martyrdom:

(a) Noble death. Early within the theology of primitive Christianity there developed a concern for the image of the devout follower of God who would sacrifice his or her own life as an expression of faith. This theme was already prominent within the general culture of the Greek world and was often applied as a positive tool for understanding the death of famous philosophers and generals. In certain respects the early interpreters of Jesus of Nazareth cast this image around the circumstances of his own death as a way to explain the horror of the cross—a form of execution reserved for only the worst of criminals. These Christians came to insist that the death of Jesus, the Son of God, was to be understood both as the ultimate devotion of a son to the will of his father and as the ultimate sacrifice of blood that was offered by God for the salvation of those accepting this sacrifice.

The death of Polycarp likewise came to be seen as a demonstration of the devotion of a loyal disciple to his master. Though encouraged to save his own life, he chose to sacrifice his body rather than his faith; though doomed to death by fire, he refused to struggle in resistance; though tempted to curse his persecutors, he chose to offer a prayer of thanks instead. The Martyrdom offers no explicit statement that Polycarp believed that he should submit to the power of the civil authorities in order to save the lives of others. The implicit message, however, clearly indicates that the bishop's desire to maintain his allegiance to Christ in the face of death should be interpreted by others as a model of faith.

(b) War between good and evil. Throughout, the Martyrdom gives the distinct impression that the persecutions that claimed the life of Polycarp were motivated by evil forces that sought to thwart the spread of God's message of salvation for the world. These forces are divided into three primary categories: the civil authorities of the Roman Empire, the Jews, and the *evil one* or the devil.

From the beginning the reader is confronted with the living reality of the persecution of Christians by the forces of Rome. Polycarp's own ordeal is introduced only in chapter 5 after the context of widespread tortures and deaths has been well established. The bishop is interrogated at first by the local captain of police, who served at the pleasure of Rome, and thereafter by the Roman proconsul in charge of the region of Smyrna. Attempts are made to compel Polycarp to "swear by Caesar" and to make a sacrifice to Rome (chapters 8–10). And it is by the power of the Roman centurions that Polycarp finally is murdered.

The local Jewish community is described as a second force that opposes God's will. In 12.3 the Jews rise up and call for Polycarp's death after he has confessed that he is a Christian. They call him the "destroyer of gods" who teaches against sacrifice and worship (12.2). And in 13.1 it is the Jews who eagerly assist in the effort to build a fire for the execution. Finally, in 17.2 and 18.1 the Jews insist that Polycarp's body must be destroyed in order that the Christians not be able to worship the corpse.

The final opponent to Polycarp is the devil himself, whom the reader is tempted to see as simply one of several forces struggling against God and the disciples of Christ. In 2.4 the reader is told that the devil used many devices of torture against the Christians. And in 16.1 those who finally execute the bishop with a sword are described as the devil's own disciples—the *men of lawlessness*. Finally, it is the evil one who ensures, according to 17.1–2, that the officials of the city follow the suggestion of the Jews to destroy Polycarp's body.

All of these forces—the Roman Empire, the Jews, the devil—strive to frustrate the will of God. Polycarp himself believed that he stood alone in the battle against these enemies and yet, though his body was destroyed, his witness remains alive to encourage others who must fight this same battle.

Several interesting images appear throughout the Martyrdom. These offer a unique glimpse into the gradually developing terminology of faith and struggle within the second-century church:

5.2.8 What special images appear?

(a) Away with the atheists (3.2; 9.2). In the Martyrdom this phrase refers to the early Christians. In this proclamation the reader discovers that in the eyes of the Romans, who worshipped many gods and goddesses, those who followed Christ were not considered to be worshipers of any god. With the use of this phrase, an interesting contrast is offered. In their frenzy to destroy those who will not revere the Roman gods, the crowds call for the execution of Polycarp in 3.2. Yet in 9.2, when Polycarp is compelled by the proconsul to cry "away with the atheists" himself, he does so. Here, however, he gestures toward the lawless crowds whom he perceives to be the followers of false gods and who, hence, are the true atheists.

(b) Prayer of Polycarp (14.1–3). Considerable scholarly attention has been given to the prayer of Polycarp occurring immediately prior to his execution. At that time when he might be expected to curse his circumstances, he instead offers praises to God. It is quite possible that this particular text was inserted into the Martyrdom as an endorsement of contemporary church traditions associated with the **eucharist** since the prayer mentions the sharing of a cup and a sacrifice which is acceptable to God. In either case, the language is highly stylized and stands apart from the wording of the remaining text. As a prayer of thanks, it serves as a worthy testimony to the memory of Polycarp's faith.

(c) Sweet aroma of a martyr's death (15.2). According to the Martyrdom, when the fire is ignited in anticipation of Polycarp's death, the flames do not consume his body but arise to form a wall which surrounds him. The reader is told that he then stands within this heat and is baked as bread. From the heat of the flames the smell of perfumes and incense emanates, as though the bishop were a precious gift prayerfully offered upon the altar to God. This imagery is depicted in order to emphasize the pleasant nature of Polycarp's sacrifice. The incredible contrast created in the mind of the reader between the anticipated stench of a burning corpse and the unexpected aroma of freshly baking bread recalls the words of Ignatius, who previously had imagined that he himself soon would be ground by wild animals to become "the pure bread of Christ" (*Romans* 4.1).

(d) Bishop of the catholic church in Smyrna (16.2). When the author praises the status of Polycarp as one of Christ's chosen disciples, the bishop is further described as the leader of a "catholic church." This is one of the earliest references to the early church as *catholic,* which means universal. Scholars believe that this text has been added in order to indicate that by the time of Polycarp the church had spread throughout the known world. Thus it had begun to develop a vague sense of unity among its individual communities. In certain respects our author takes advantage of this moment to establish that the church in Smyrna stood within a solid tradition through its association with Polycarp, a bishop referred to as "an apostolic and prophetic teacher" whose leadership gave a certain aura of authority to the community that he served. This reverence of Polycarp would undoubtedly have raised the congregation of Smyrna to a preferred status among the local churches and would have assisted its leaders in defining the nature of orthodox theology for many early Christians.

(e) Birthday of a martyr (18.3). Toward the end of our text the author remarks upon the *birthday* of Polycarp's martyrdom. In this passage the reader is told that the date of the bishop's death has become a kind of anniversary which is remembered within the early church and honored with gladness and joy. Already our author has admitted that the followers of Polycarp had begun to reverence the bishop himself prior to his death, so that he remained fully clothed until the point of execution since "the faithful were zealous . . . to touch his flesh" (13.2). At another level, the reference to a birthday illustrates the growing realization among early Christians that martyrdom on behalf of Christ was not an end to life itself, but was a rebirth into another existence—a second birthday as it were. Similar comparisons arose in later literature, as illustrated by the theologian **Origen,** who associated martyrdom with the ritual of baptism. Baptism itself was viewed by the church as a form of rebirth for converts to Christianity.

5.2.9 How does the text relate to scripture?

Because the Martyrdom is offered as the report of a historical event, the author does not feel compelled to engage either in the extensive use of scripture or in any extended discussion of specific biblical themes. This observation holds true both with respect to the Old Testament **canon** and to those writings designated by the later church as the New Testament.

We can assume that the author was fully aware of such texts. In the case of the Old Testament, it would be only natural in light of the accusations against the Jews—that is, that they were, at least in part, responsible for Polycarp's execution—that there would be no desire to turn to the scriptures of the Jews as a ready source of reflection and interpretation with respect to the bishop's death. It is true, of course, that the Letter of Barnabas utilizes Old Testament texts to condemn the purported beliefs of contemporary Judaism. But the author of the Martyrdom reveals no such inclination.

As to New Testament writings cited in the letter, these are scattered and few. The most obvious examples include the blessing at the end of the introduction (see Jude 2), the charge to think always of others in 1.2 (see Philippians 2:4), the recollection of the mystical visions of the martyrs in 2.3 (see 1 Corinthians 2:9), the warning that Christians should not seek martyrdom in 4.1 (see Matthew 10:23), the account of Polycarp's submission to the authorities in 7.1 (see Acts 21:14), and the observation that governing authorities receive their power from God in 10.2 (see Romans 13:1 and 1 Peter 2:13–14).

In the case of the Martyrdom, however, the picture of Polycarp's execution is cast into a broader biblical image than can be constructed by individual passages from scripture. From beginning to end, the bishop's arrest, trial, and execution are painted against the canvas of similar events in the life of Jesus of Nazareth as they are recorded in the New Testament gospels. Thus it is that Polycarp serves as the host for a final meal, and agonizes in prayer immediately prior to his arrest by the authorities. He is escorted into the city on a donkey, is interrogated by an important Roman authority, and is then condemned to death with the eager agreement of the Jews. Although he is condemned to the flames, his body is pierced to ensure that he has died. All of these images are compared to the final days of Jesus' life in Jerusalem. Each image, in turn, is then recast according to the final hours of Polycarp's life in Smyrna. As the author states in 1.2, Polycarp waited to be betrayed as had the Lord. In 6.2, the bishop is brought to the arena for trial in order to participate in the fate of Jesus, just as his betrayers were to share in the punishment of Judas Iscariot, who previously betrayed his master.

The close reading of Polycarp's execution alongside of Jesus' death would argue against the probability that the Martyrdom is an accurate narration of historical events. Yet in the experience of second-century Christians, the transfer of this poignant imagery—from the death of God's chosen messiah, Jesus, to the death of God's favored bishop, Polycarp—was a magnificent use of a biblical theme which served to reassure faithful believers everywhere of the authentic nature of the apostolic tradition as it was experienced in the witness of the church at Smyrna.

Figure 5–B — GOSPEL PARALLELS BETWEEN THE DEATHS OF JESUS AND POLYCARP

Gospel event	Gospel text	Parallel in Martyrdom
Jesus enters Jerusalem on a donkey	Matthew 21:1–11	Polycarp enters Smyrna on a donkey (8.1)
Prayer for the disciples	John 17:1–26	Prayer for the churches (5.1)
Betrayal by a disciple	Matthew 26:47–49	Betrayal within household (6.1–2)
Host at a final meal	Matthew 26:17–29	Host at a final meal (7.2)
Prayer before the arrest	Matthew 26:36–46	Prayer before the arrest (7.2–3)
Interrogation by Herod	Luke 23:6–12	Interrogation by Herod (8.2–3)
Jesus identified as "the man"	John 19:5	Polycarp told by a voice from heaven to "be a man" (9.1)
Pilate questions Jesus	John 18:28–19:11	Proconsul tries Polycarp (9.2–10.1)
Jews call for Jesus' death	John 19:12–16	Jews call for Polycarp's death (12.2–13.1)
Crucifixion on a Friday	Luke 23:54	Crucifixion on a Friday (7.1)
Body taken for burial	Matthew 27:57–61	Bones taken for safety (18.2–3)

5.3   CONTENTS

Outline of the Materials

Summary of the
Argument

Mercy, peace, and love to the church at Philomelium. We wished to write to you about the last of the martyrdoms—that of the bishop Polycarp.

According to God's will, the noble martyrs of Christ have suffered through many acts of torture at the hands of the devil. Some, like Germanicus, have endured with honor; others, like Quintus, have submitted to the will of Caesar. Our noble bishop Polycarp was not alarmed when he heard of these events, though his friends eventually convinced him to flee to the countryside. There he prayed and saw his own death in a vision. Thus it was no surprise when he ultimately was betrayed to the authorities. Yet even when men came to arrest him late at night, he offered them a meal out of his hospitality.

On the way to the arena for his trial the authorities tried to persuade him to submit to Caesar, but he refused. In the arena itself the proconsul charged the bishop three times to reject Christ and to sacrifice to Caesar, with the threat of a cruel death if he did not! Yet Polycarp spurned them and boldly proclaimed "I am a Christian" before his accusers. At this the crowds cried out for him to meet his end with a lion. But since such contests are no longer performed here, the aged Polycarp was condemned to be burned alive.

The wood was quickly prepared and Polycarp did not resist. Indeed, he was never secured to a post since he willingly promised to submit to the flames. And, just like a sheep prepared for some sacrifice, he stood and offered praise to God. But when the wood was lit, the flames formed a protective shell around him and did not burn his flesh. So the executioner struck him with a sword and from his body came a dove together with so much blood that the flames were extinguished! And to ensure that we would not revere the body itself, it was burned by the authorities. Thus we now have only the precious bones of the bishop as a glorious memory of his martyrdom. In this way the blessed Polycarp became the twelfth martyr of Smyrna, a true follower of the gospel and a champion over evil.

It is Marcion who brings you this word—please send our letter on to those who desire it. We offer our greetings to you.

Polycarp was martyred seven days before a great sabbath, on the twenty-second [or twenty-third] of February, when Philip of Tralles was high priest and Statius Quadratus was proconsul.

In the name of Jesus Christ, we offer our best wishes to those who follow the gospel teachings.

I, Socrates, copied this text of Gaius in Corinth, who acquired it from Polycarp's own disciple Irenaeus.

I, Pionius, recopied this text from a worn copy because Polycarp himself revealed it to me in a vision.

[From the Moscow Codex] Gaius copied this text from Irenaeus, who was a student of Polycarp and remembered that the bishop had rebuked the false teacher Marcion with the words "I recognize you as the firstborn of Satan." Thus it is that I, Pionius, copied this text from Isocrates, who used the text of Gaius which was copied from Irenaeus.

5.4 RELATED LITERATURE

Barnes, T. D. "A Note on Polycarp." *Journal of Theological Studies* New Series 18 (3, 1967), pp. 433–37.

———. "Pre-Decian *Acta Martyrum*." *Journal of Theological Studies* New Series 19 (4, 1968), pp. 510–14.

Baumeister, T. "Martyrdom and Persecution in Early Christianity." *Concilium* 163 (1, 1983), pp. 3–8.

Cadoux, Cecil John. *Ancient Smyrna: A History of the City from the Earliest Times to 324 A.D.* Oxford: Basil Blackwell, 1938. (DS51.S7.C3 1938)

Carroll, Howard. "Polycarp of Smyrna with Special Reference to Early Christian Martyrdom." Ph.D. dissertation. Duke University, 1946.

Frend, W. H. C. *Martyrdom and Persecution in the Early Church.* Pages 268–302. Oxford: Basil Blackwell, 1965. (BQX255.F7 1965)

Robinson, J. Armitage. "The 'Apostolic Anaphora' and the Prayer of St. Polycarp." *Journal of Theological Studies* 21 (1, 1920), pp. 97–105.

Schoedel, William R. *Polycarp, Martyrdom of Polycarp, Fragments of Papias.* Pages 3–49. The Apostolic Fathers 5. New York: Thomas Nelson & Sons, 1965. (BQ1080.A4 1964)

Telfer, W. "The Date of the Martyrdom of Polycarp." *Journal of Theological Studies* New Series 3 (1, 1952), pp. 79–83.

Tripp, David. "The Prayer of St Polycarp and the Development of Anaphoral Prayer." *Ephemerides Liturgicae* 104 (1, 1990), pp. 97–132.

6 The First Letter of Clement of Rome to the Corinthians (1 Clement)

6.1 ANSWERS

6.2 QUESTIONS

6.2.1 Where did we get our text?

The text of 1 Clement remains for us today in manuscripts written in Greek, Latin, Coptic, and Syriac. All of the available texts retain some value, of course, since each bears witness to an aspect of the long tradition of the text's circulation in the church. Nonetheless, there is no question that the Greek manuscripts are the most important among these documents, primarily because they preserve the original language of the text and appear to reflect fewer alterations by the various scribes who copied the letter throughout the centuries. The other texts tend to suffer from certain omissions and changes, as is illustrated by our single Latin version. Scholars have come to believe that it was altered in order to promote the authority of the bishop of Rome among the early churches. The manuscripts including 1 Clement are as follows:

(a) There are two examples of the Greek edition of the letter. These Greek witnesses are contained in important collections of ancient Christian materials.

The first copy of the Greek text appears in the well-known manuscript of **Codex Alexandrinus.** This document, which dates from the fifth century, is one of our most important biblical manuscripts. Given to the patriarch of the church at Alexandria in 1098, the **codex** was eventually presented to King Charles I of England in 1627 and now belongs to the collection of texts at the British Library in London. That portion of the manuscript which preserves 1 Clement is complete, with the exception of a single, missing leaf (or page) which would have contained the materials of 57.7–63.4.

The other Greek manuscript, and undoubtedly the more important of the two, is the **Codex Hierosolymitanus.** Discovered in 1873 in Constantinople (modern Istanbul) by Archbishop Philotheos Bryennios, this text contains our only complete Greek witness to the text of 1 Clement. The **codex** is extremely important to research in the apostolic fathers in general since it also preserves several others texts in the collection. As scholars have often noted, there is a great value to the fact that several writings from the apostolic fathers have been preserved together in a single manuscript. When the writings in **Codex Hierosolymitanus** are compared against other versions, it becomes possible to identify the tendencies of the scribe who copied the **codex** and, thus, to determine where the scribe has likely made changes to the manuscript tradition.

(b) The text of 1 Clement also appears in a single Latin translation. Although this particular manuscript comes from the eleventh century, scholars believe that the version of 1 Clement it preserves dates to the second or third century. As mentioned above, however, it is generally thought that this text was unfortunately corrupted sometime around the ninth or tenth century in order to promote the importance of the bishop of Rome, or the pope.

(c) There is also a twelfth-century Syriac manuscript containing 1 Clement. The manuscript apparently is a translation based upon an earlier Greek text. Its scribe was careful in the process of translation, yet the differences in the languages do not provide for an accurate reconstruction of the original Greek text. For example, it is impossible to determine the actual order of the original Greek wording. It seems that the translator was forced to alter or explain difficult Greek readings.

(d) Of the two Coptic papyrus texts, one comes from the fourth century and the other from the fifth century. While these manuscripts are early, both unfortunately are incomplete. The fourth-century manuscript omits 34.6–42.2, while the latter ends at 26.2. Once again, it is difficult to determine how accurately these translations represent the original Greek text.

(e) In addition to the editions of 1 Clement preserved in specific manuscripts, the text is known from fragments and quotations throughout early Christian literature. The oldest of these quotations has been preserved in Polycarp's letter to the Philippians at 9.2. The letter of 1 Clement was also widely used in the work of **Clement of Alexandria** from the early third century. Later, it became an important source for other ancient Alexandrian authors, such as Clement's student, **Origen,** as well as **Didymus the Blind.** In his *Ecclesiastical History,* **Eusebius of Caesarea** observed that several early Christian bishops appear to have held 1 Clement in high esteem. **Eusebius** himself summarizes the letter in this same place.

Many early authors regarded 1 Clement as inspired and, as is evident from the testimony of **Clement of Alexandria,** thought it should be part of the canon of sacred scripture. Though 1 Clement was popular throughout the Eastern church, it was less widely used in the West. **Jerome,** who was familiar with the text from its importance in Rome, quotes 1 Clement throughout his commentaries. In general, however, Western authors made little use of the letter. With the advent of the Medieval period, 1 Clement was practically forgotten. In the East, where it had been so popular earlier, its orthodoxy eventually was questioned. With time its emphasis upon the importance of Rome led to its gradual abandonment.

As with the writings of Ignatius, the text of 1 Clement is an ancient letter sent from the leaders of one Christian community to those of another. Here the reader discovers the various literary units in most early Christian letters: an introduction (preface), the reason for the letter (1.1), a section of appreciation and thanks for the reader (1.2–2.8), an extensive body or main message of the author (3.1–61.3), and concluding greetings (62.1–65.2). The most striking feature in the structure of 1 Clement is the extensive length of the main body of the letter. Unlike the letters of Paul in the New Testament, or even of the writings of Ignatius and Polycarp, the main section of 1 Clement is quite extensive and incorporates numerous images to develop its primary thesis.

First Clement's blend of two basic, yet different, literary styles makes it an intriguing document. Scholars often note that the author extensively uses ancient Greek diatribe—a literary technique that constructs an imaginary conversation, typically containing rhetorical questions, in order to guide the reader to a particular conclusion concerning a specific topic. Arguments in ancient Greek and Latin literature commonly took this literary form. At the same time, the author incorporates a common form of Jewish scriptural interpretation. This approach, generally recognized as the *synagogue homily* style, typically begins with some text from scripture, and thereafter links additional passages through common words and phrases in order to build support for a given idea. The blend of these two literary forms—Greek diatribe and Jewish synagogue homily—already may be discovered in the approach of Paul throughout his New Testament letters. In the case of both Paul and 1 Clement, one finds a blend of two distinct cultures in which both perspectives are freely used, and yet neither dominates.

6.2.2 What form does the text take?

The title of the text of 1 Clement in Greek and Latin manuscripts is "The Letter of Clement to the Corinthians." Coptic and Syriac evidence places the author in Rome, and the Syriac further asserts that the sender is Clement. This combined evidence logically indicates that someone named Clement occupied a position in the church of Rome that authorized him to write to the church in Corinth. This may suggest either that he was a leader of the community in Rome or that he had been commissioned by the authorities

6.2.3 Who was the author?

there to pen the letter. The issue of authorship in the case of 1 Clement actually revolves around the question of whether the authority behind the text came from a bishop or, instead, from a council of ruling presbyters who did not endorse a single community leader. Each of these options requires some specific consideration:

(a) Authorship based upon the authority of a bishop. Ancient tradition often assumed that the authority of the letter stemmed from the figure of a man named Clement who was the bishop of Rome in the closing years of the first century. There is some disagreement as to the place which this Clement held in the developing **episcopacy** of the community in Rome. The issue revolves around whether Clement was the second bishop of the city or, instead, if one follows the traditional assumption that the apostle Peter was the first bishop, whether Clement was third in succession. Both the late second-century bishop **Irenaeus** (of Lyons) and **Eusebius of Caesarea** believed that Clement was the third bishop of Rome. While there are no records from the period which could verify that Clement was a bishop of Rome in any case, the testimony of **Irenaeus** and **Eusebius** appear to support such a tradition.

If this assumption is accepted, then it is necessary to ask who this Clement may have been. No ancient testimony speaks directly about the person of Clement. Consequently, any definite statements about his place of birth and death are not available. Nevertheless, scholars have raised some considerations in this respect that merit attention.

Sources indicate that a cousin of the emperor **Domitian,** named Titus Flavius Clemens, lived during the late first century. Our Clement may have been a freedman who was attached to the house of Clemens or, possibly, was Clemens himself. **Domitian** evidently thought enough of Titus Flavius Clemens to give him his niece in marriage and, thereafter, to designate the sons of Clemens to be heirs of the empire. After a year of service in the office of consul, a high government position, Clemens was accused of impiety and fell from favor. This accusation indicates that he no longer chose to worship the gods of the Roman Empire and may imply that he elected to follow the God of the Christians. Clemens was eventually executed by the state for atheism. If this scenario is correct, then this man might very well have been the author of our letter—Clement, bishop of Rome. The implications of such a connection would include the astounding realization that Christianity had penetrated the highest levels of society within only a generation or two after its humble beginnings in Palestine.

Unfortunately, there is little explicit evidence connecting Titus Flavius Clemens with 1 Clement. The single supporting detail within the text of 1 Clement occurs in the prayer of chapters 59–61. This prayer includes a blessing for those who rule over the nations of the earth (see 60.4–61.2), and may have come from someone who was concerned for the government of Rome in a personal sense. If our author was indeed Titus Flavius Clemens or a member of his household, then it would be logical that such a prayer for civil leaders would be included within the letter.

(b) Authorship based upon the authority of multiple leaders. Nowhere in the letter is the author's name revealed. From the outset the letter begins with an address to the church at Corinth from the church at Rome, but there is no mention of any particular individual. In the Coptic editions of the letter, the text concludes with the title "The Epistle of the Romans to the Corinthians," and again no specific author is mentioned.

Numerous scholars have noted that there is no firm evidence to suggest that the church in Rome at the turn of the first century was lead by a single authority, such as a bishop. Indeed, the author of the letter is continually cited in the plural as *we* or *us*, which does not suggest that a single individual served as the authority behind the text. Furthermore, chapter 44 speaks as though the community was led by a number of persons—perhaps a circle of elders, or presbyters. The position of presbyter was well-known throughout the early churches and was occupied by persons responsible for the affairs of the community with respect to worship, organization, and public relations. It is quite possible that the community at Rome itself was directed by such a circle of persons during the early decades of its existence.

Within such a circle there would naturally have been a leader, of course, though this would not necessarily have been a person with authority or powers distinct from those of the remaining members of the group. Such a person, a leader of the presbyters, may in fact have been the author of our text—perhaps someone named Clement. Or, perhaps, this Clement may have been an important scribe within the Roman church who composed the letter on behalf of the presbyters.

6.2.4 When was the text written?	Several distinct pieces of evidence suggest a date for 1 Clement toward the end of the first century. **Eusebius of Caesarea** places the **episcopacy** of the bishop Clement during the reign of the Roman emperor **Domitian** (AD 81–96). The author considers the age of the New Testament apostles to have been concluded (see chapters 42–44). And the presbyters mentioned in chapter 44, those supposedly appointed by the apostles, are depicted as near the end of their lives.

Furthermore, the letter begins with a mention of the recent misfortunes and calamities that prevented the church at Rome from replying promptly to the questions previously raised by the church at Corinth. Certain scholars suggest that the mention of these calamities is a veiled reference to the repressive reign of the emperor **Nero,** who ruled during the years AD 54–68. But the allusion to the executions of the apostles Peter and Paul (under **Nero**) in chapter 5 suggests that this particular reign of terror had long since passed. Other scholars think these misfortunes indicate that certain recent persecutions had occurred in Rome. The reign of the ruthless **Domitian,** or the short rule of his successor **Nerva** (ruled 96–98), certainly would have provided an atmosphere for such persecutions. Yet a third group of scholars argues that this strife was internal to the church itself, and thus was not a general persecution of the congregation by some outside threat. If this final interpretation is accurate, then the text of 1 Clement could have been composed at some point after the reign of **Domitian.** That the letter was written many years after the death of **Domitian** is unlikely, however, since evidence exists that Polycarp (died ca. 156) knew of the text.

The widest range of dates during which 1 Clement could have been composed would thus feature the years 81–110. There is no solid reason to deny that the letter was composed during the reign of the emperor **Domitian** himself.

6.2.5 In what setting was the text written?	The modern reader of 1 Clement must certainly question why the church at Corinth should have sought to resolve its internal crisis through the agency of the church at Rome. Unlike the powerful church in Rome of later years, the first-century Roman church had not achieved supremacy concerning questions of doctrine and faith. Christian communities throughout the empire did not typically look

toward Rome for deciding matters of theology and organization. The city of Rome undoubtedly attained stature as the place where Peter and Paul were martyred, and, of course, it was the political and economic center of the empire. It is even possible that the congregation in Rome was recognized as a first among equals by the end of the first century, though this is difficult to establish. In either case, the exclusive nature of Rome's authority in terms of the Christian faith was not generally recognized.

The city of Corinth itself has an interesting history. From its founding until 146 BC, Corinth was a thriving Greek city. It was destroyed by the Romans in 146 and refounded as a Roman colony on the same site by Julius Caesar in the year 44 BC. Because of its strategic importance, it became the capital of the province of Achaia. Corinth was situated on an isthmus, which gave it two seaports and caused the city to become a great commercial center. Because of its economic importance, many of Corinth's citizens became wealthy. The city attracted a fairly large Jewish population, and subsequently it became a center for early Christian missionary activity. Converted Jews and pagans often supported the missionary efforts of the church there. Corinth assumed the characteristics of its Roman founders with respect to its society, political structure, and general culture. Because of their Roman heritage, the Corinthians were especially attached to the city of Rome. They looked toward Rome as a model and supported Roman government and the Roman way of life. It was only logical, therefore, that the Christians of Corinth would have turned to Rome for the answers to their questions.

Of course, Corinth was a vibrant center of Christianity in its own right. The revered apostle Paul had founded the church there around the year AD 54, and he wrote letters to the Corinthians which, in time, would be regarded as inspired. But it undoubtedly was the significance of the community in Corinth itself which created problems for the leadership of the church there. Indeed, Paul's letters previously had been concerned with the issue of divisions within the Corinthian church. Now, some forty to fifty years later, the subject of division had returned.

At the beginning of 1 Clement (1.1) the author mentions that the letter is a reply to questions from Corinth. The specific nature of these questions is not provided, but it is possible to reconstruct the concerns of the Corinthians from the context of the letter itself. It

6.2.6 Why was the text written?

appears, for example, that the established order of church society in Corinth had been disrupted. The well-respected presbyters of the community had been deposed, or at least challenged, by younger members of the community. The aftermath was a community of divided loyalties and fragile unity. It was to this community situation that 1 Clement was directed.

The purpose of 1 Clement thus appears to be clear. The church at Corinth was in turmoil and the church at Rome was concerned to reestablish order within the community. Scholars have proposed two primary themes:

(a) Many scholars think that the central theme of the letter is *order*. In support of this belief, they discern a heavy influence of the ancient Greek philosophy of **Stoicism.** The author is seen to apply this understanding to the Judeo-Christian tradition. As an illustration of this philosophy, the author insists that the God of Christian faith is the creator of order. All of creation has its time and place. The seasons come and go according to a cycle that is carefully determined by God's will. God has revealed this will through the prophets and, more recently and perfectly, through Jesus Christ. As a participant in God's world, humanity cannot ignore the order within the world itself. Just as nature is ordered, so too is humanity. The order within the church in Corinth had been disrupted, and it had thus offended God. Therefore, it was paramount to reestablish the divine order within that community.

(b) The second theme emphasizes the need to restore *peace*. Scholars identifying this theme argue that the author wished to voice the specific views of the community in Rome, which was primarily Jewish in orientation. The Roman church would have been less interested in the influence of Greek philosophy on interpretations of God, and would have preferred that the Corinthians recognize the need to endorse scriptural authority and remain obedient to the will of God as expressed by the Old Testament prophets. At all costs, it was necessary to preserve peace.

While these two approaches reach similar conclusions, the difference in their focus derives from the presumed nature of the church at Rome. Was the Roman community in basic support of a Jewish-Christian theology, or was there more of a Greek influence at work? There are good reasons to argue either way. Ultimately, however, there is no need to choose one of these themes to the exclusion of the other since the question of order and peace could have been of equal interest to the author.

The text of 1 Clement contains several prominent features that distinguish it from other Christian literature of the period. In a basic sense, each of these is related to the author's understanding of who Jesus of Nazareth was in his role as the Christ of Christian faith. The role of Christology in the thought of the author can hardly be exaggerated, since it is within this context that the numerous images from scripture and pagan traditions are offered. The Christology of 1 Clement, while not developed by the standards of later church councils, is more explicit than other contemporary documents. The following elements of the letter should be viewed against this concern for Christology:

6.2.7 What are the primary traits of the text?

(a) Christ associated with God. The text includes an unusual number of instances associating the figures of God and Jesus by name and function. For instance, the term *Lord* occurs almost fifty times in reference to God the Father alone. Yet the same term also refers nineteen times to Jesus. The letter emphasizes numerous references both to the Lord Jesus and to the Lord Jesus Christ (though never to the Lord Christ), so that there is no doubt as to the theological importance of Jesus as the Son of God within the mind-set of the Roman church. Additional references to Jesus by name—either as Jesus Christ or simply as Christ—appear fifty-one times. When the author describes the actions of God, the name of God and that of Jesus are employed interchangeably. Thus it is that at the very beginning of the letter the author confesses that grace and peace come from God through Jesus. This constant association of God with Jesus reflects an emerging understanding of the divine relationship between God the Father and Jesus the Son.

(b) Christ as a model. Apart from the high theological respect attributed to the figure of Jesus, the text also focuses upon Jesus as a teacher and as an example to be followed. During the years between the composition of the Old and New Testaments, it was commonly believed that divine intermediaries (or angels) bridged the gap between God and humanity. It is apparent that Jesus, as a teacher and prophet, occupied this role for our author. In this respect, the author comes very close to an understanding of Jesus as a divine emissary from God who had extended the offer of salvation to those who would accept it. At the same time, however, this teaching does not slip into the doctrines of **gnosticism,** which taught that the message of Jesus was for only a select few. Most important in this light are the teaching and example of Jesus with regard to humility and obedience. This image of a humble, obedient Jesus is the example to be imitated by the Corinthians.

(c) Christ as the scepter of God (16.2). Another key image of Jesus painted by the author is "scepter of God," a title which reveals the supreme dignity of the person of Jesus. The scepter, or staff of royal authority, has symbolized the power of earthly rulers since antiquity. In the mind of our author, Jesus himself has the power and authority of God and, as such, can bring salvation to God's kingdom—the world.

A more profound issue concerns the early Christian understanding of who Jesus was. The humanity of Jesus was not an issue for the believers in Rome. Instead, the divine nature of Jesus as God's chosen messiah (= christ) was the issue. Our author states that Jesus came into the world by humble means, yet he could have rightfully come in majesty. This theology echoes the apostle Paul in his New Testament letter to the Philippians. In Philippians 2:6–11, Paul uses an ancient Christian hymn to insist that Christ came from God. Yet Christ did not come in majesty, but in lowliness he humbled himself unto death. In 2 Corinthians 8:9, Paul employed a similar idea: "For you know the generous act of our Lord Jesus Christ, that though he was rich, yet for your sakes he became poor, so that by his poverty you might become rich." Since Paul already had written to the Corinthians in this way, it was only logical that the author of 1 Clement would imitate Paul. Paul had become a revered figure in Corinth, and an appeal to the apostle's teaching in order to press the importance of the Roman message would be effective. The fact that 1 Clement accepts a concept of a christ who existed prior to the creation of the world undoubtedly indicates that the Roman community in general supported such a theology by the end of the first century.

(d) Christ as a sign of order. The focus upon Christology may also have functioned to impress upon the Corinthians the importance of order within the church. This appears in the image of the relationship of church authority to the figure of Christ and, in return, the relationship of Christ to God. First Clement 42.1 evidences Rome's view of the descending order of authority that should characterize the Christian community. God gave Christ lordship, and Christ in turn gave authority to his apostles. The apostles subsequently gave authority to the bishops they appointed in each city as they proclaimed the message of the gospel. Once again, the writer appeals to a divinely sanctioned established order and presumes to have the authority to replace any elements of disorder within a church community.

(e) The death of Christ for all people. The imagery of blood and death figures prominently in the author's Christology. Jesus is depicted as a suffering servant who freely died for the salvation of all people. This suffering servant image, which is drawn from the book of Isaiah in the Old Testament, reflects the ancient belief that a sacrifice can be offered to God on behalf of an entire nation. Since blood was believed to contain a creature's life force, the shedding of blood through sacrifice symbolized total submission to God. For the Israelites, the sacrifice of an animal symbolized this submission. Throughout the New Testament, however, the blood of Jesus himself is viewed in this role.

The text of 1 Clement uses the imagery of blood four times. The first use of blood imagery occurs at 7.4, where the author states that Christ's death affords all of humanity the opportunity for reconciliation with God. Through the death of Jesus the world is provided with an opportunity for repentance. At 12.7 the image of blood is combined with the theme of obedience to encourage order. Just as the prostitute Rahab in the Old Testament book of Joshua hung a red banner from her window in order to be saved from death at the hands of the invading Israelites, so those who believe (as did Rahab) in the gospel will be saved by the blood of Christ (the red banner). At 21.6 the author writes of the order of the universe which had been established in virtue by God. The reverence of Christ, who shed his blood in obedience to God's order, thus becomes the model of obedience for all people. The final image of blood occurs at 49.6. Here the Corinthians are reminded that the shedding of blood occurred in order to recall the love of God for humanity. As God has loved humanity, so Jesus also expressed this love through his death.

(f) The resurrection of Christ. First Clement speaks explicitly about the resurrection of Christ and its importance for the salvation of humanity. Consistent with the theme of order, the author indicates the presence of this image in creation in order to show that nature itself foreshadows the resurrection. Beginning with 24.2, 1 Clement connects the cycles of nature—day gives way to night but then returns in the morning, seeds fall to the ground only to die and grow into plant-bearing fruits. The event of Christ's resurrection was entirely consistent with the order of nature and the will of God.

This imagery then brings the author to comment about the significance of the resurrection for daily life. The resurrection is a promise to be fulfilled. At the general resurrection of the dead, those who lived justly will be vindicated while evildoers will be punished. First Clement does not anticipate that God's eternal kingdom will come at the present moment but, rather, that it will arrive at a later, indefinite time. This *later* theme is consistent with the author's view that Jesus' death was not so much a sign of the imminent kingdom of God but a means for evoking the repentance of humanity.

6.2.8 What special images appear?

The text contains several secondary images that give 1 Clement a special character among early Christian writings. Included among these are the following elements:

(a) A citizenship worthy of Christ (3.4). The author reflects a growing realization among early Christians that a religious loyalty to the community of Christ was not necessarily a denial of loyalty toward the demands of secular authority. This idea finds parallels in the Letter of Polycarp, the Shepherd of Hermas, and the Letter to Diognetus, and is developed even more extensively by later theologians. Yet it is especially important that the motif appears in 1 Clement, since the community of Rome would have been forced by its geographical location at the heart of the Roman Empire to decide quite early whether it could live in harmony with the Roman government. In his New Testament letter to the church at Rome, the apostle Paul had already called upon the community to subject itself to the authorities (see 13:1–8), and this theme is clearly repeated in 1 Clement 60.4–61.2 in a prayer on behalf of the Corinthians. It is not by accident, therefore, that our author views order and obedience as necessary components of the living community of Christ.

(b) The phoenix. Chapter 25 of the letter features a story about the phoenix, a mythical bird from ancient Egyptian folklore. According to the story, the phoenix was a fantastic bird of fire which lived for a period of five hundred years, after which it built a tomb and died. From this tomb there would arise a worm, a creature which fed upon the carcass of the dead bird, sprouted wings, and then carried the bones of its parent to their eternal resting place at the Egyptian site of Heliopolis—which means *city of the sun*. The new creature then would return to repeat the five-hundred year cycle. Our author employs this story of the phoenix as a sign of the resurrection. Just as the seed dies and sprouts new life from the ground (see 24.4–5), so too was the phoenix believed to gain new life from the remains of its former existence. This imagery depicts the reality of the resurrection of Jesus and its testimony that life derives from death according to the order established by God.

(c) Jesus Christ—both priest and sacrifice. Early Christian literature does not generally utilize priestly imagery, such as one finds in first-century Judaism, as a means of understanding Christianity's relationship with Judaism. The primary exception to this in the New Testament occurs in the book of Hebrews. Specifically, in one passage the author of Hebrews calls Jesus "the great high priest" who sacrifices to God on behalf of his people (4:14–5:10). Yet at the same time, the author of Hebrews describes Jesus as the ultimate sacrifice for all peoples (9:23–10:18). This dual role of Jesus—both as the priest who sacrifices and as the sacrifice itself—reappears in the theology of 1 Clement. The image of the sacrifice, of Jesus as God's son whose blood has been spilled for human salvation, has been discussed above (see page 109). The image of Jesus as a high priest who acts on behalf of his people is developed in 1 Clement through the use of three distinct images: as high priest Jesus offers support for human weaknesses (see 36.1 and 61.3); the high priest, priests, and Levites of Judaism are depicted as those in charge of the religious community, which perhaps reflects the Christian offices of bishop, presbyter, and deacon (see 40.5); and the functions of church life are demonstrated to have their center in the figure of the high priest (see 41.5). There is little question that the author of 1 Clement borrows heavily from the symbolism of the book of Hebrews, and has pressed the imagery of high priest and sacrifice into service for theology in the church at Rome.

6.2.9 How does the text relate to scripture?

From the outset, it is obvious that the letter of 1 Clement refers frequently to Old Testament scripture. The casual reader cannot help but be impressed by the author's extensive and diverse knowledge of this collection of texts. The letter draws materials from the books of Genesis, Numbers, Deuteronomy, Joshua, 1 Samuel, Esther, Job, Psalms, Proverbs, Isaiah, Jeremiah, and Ezekiel, as well as the books of Judith, Wisdom of Solomon, and Sirach from the **Apocrypha**.

Some scholars contend that the author of 1 Clement, much like the author of the Letter of Barnabas, has perhaps used an anthology of Old Testament literature. Such anthologies, or **testimonia**, were formed when materials relating to a common theme were extracted from diverse scriptural texts and combined into a single collection.

The early church often used these collections as a resource for preparing homilies or sermons. The presence of **testimonia** behind 1 Clement is further suggested by composite quotations, or groups of materials, that have been taken from their original Old Testament settings and applied to different circumstances.

Figure 6-A — BIBLICAL NAMES CITED IN 1 CLEMENT

Name	Text	Biblical Source	Theme
Cain & Abel	4.1–7	Genesis 4:3–8	jealousy divides
Jacob & Esau	4.8	Genesis 27:41–28:5	jealousy divides
Joseph	4.9	Genesis 37	jealousy divides
Moses & Pharaoh	4.10	Exodus 2:14	jealousy divides
Aaron & Miriam	4.11	Numbers 12	jealousy divides
Dathan & Abiram	4.12	Numbers 16:1–35	jealousy divides
David & Saul	4.13	1 Samuel 18–31	jealousy divides
Peter	5.4	Acts 5; 12	jealousy kills
Paul	5.5–7	Acts 14–28	jealousy kills
Noah	7.6	Genesis 7	repentance saves
Jonah	7.7	Jonah 3	repentance saves
Enoch	9.3	Genesis 5:24	obedience saves
Noah	9.4	Genesis 7	obedience saves
Abraham	10.1–7	Genesis 12–25	faith saves
Lot	11.1–2	Genesis 19	piety saves
Rahab	12.1–7	Joshua 2	hospitality saves
Elijah & Elisha	17.1	1 Kings 17–2 Kings 13	Christ foretold
Ezekiel	17.2	Ezekiel	Christ foretold
Abraham	17.3–4	Genesis 18:27	humility saves
Job	17.3–4	Job 1:1; 14:4–5	purity saves
David	18.1–17	Psalm 89:20; 51:1–17	humility saves
Abraham	31.2	Genesis 21:17	faith saves
Isaac	31.3	Genesis 22	faith saves
Jacob & Laban	31.4	Genesis 28–31	humility saves
Moses	43.1–6	Numbers 12:7; 17	order desirable
Daniel, Ananias, Azaria, Misael	45.6–7	Daniel 6:16–24	persecution comes
Paul	47.1–7	1 Corinthians 1:10	division destroys
David	52.1–4	Psalm 69:30–32; 50–51	confess sins
Moses	53.1–5	Deuteronomy 9	ask forgiveness
Judith	55.4–5	Judith 8–14	sacrifice self will
Esther	55.6	Esther 7	sacrifice self will

First Clement enlists a number of Old Testament texts. And the way in which those materials have been assembled is impressive. Unlike Ignatius, our author rarely selects a single passage as the basis for discussion about some Christian theme, such as correct doctrine or appropriate church structure. At the same time, the author does not casually compile texts as random *proof texts* for an argument that is often remote from the nature of those texts—a use of scripture that is typical of the Letter of Barnabas. Instead, 1 Clement is created from carefully selected passages of scripture that form coherent, extensive arguments in support of the author's message concerning order and peace. There is little question that this individual both knows the Old Testament materials and understands how they can best be employed.

The author also relies upon numerous writings that eventually became part of the New Testament. A review of these writings reveals that our author makes virtually no use of the New Testament Gospels. On the one hand, this is not necessarily surprising, since these texts were written toward the end of the first century and thus would not have been in widespread circulation by the time that 1 Clement was composed. On the other hand, the omission of materials from the gospels is especially curious since ancient Christian tradition assumed that the Gospel of Mark was itself composed at Rome.

Scholars sometimes note that the few gospel passages 1 Clement does use most resemble materials in the Gospel of Matthew. If our author did indeed know the text of Matthew, then this suggests some connection between the church of Rome and the church of Antioch in Syria, the city where scholars most commonly argue that the Gospel of Matthew was composed. The large Jewish communities in both Rome and Antioch may explain this connection since the fact that the author of Matthew held Jewish laws and traditions in high regard would have endeared the gospel to such settings. There is not really enough evidence, however, to confirm that our author used the Gospel of Matthew as a source. It is much more likely that the words of Jesus which appear in 1 Clement were borrowed from sayings that circulated freely among early Christian communities.

Finally, many of the letters in the New Testament seem to have been known by our author. This is especially true with respect to the letters of Paul since Pauline images are scattered throughout 1 Clement. Many scholars also point to the letter of James and observe the similarity between the theologies of James and 1 Clement. For example, issues of authority, obedience, and the importance of church structure concern both authors. While it is difficult to know to what extent our author had access to any of the New Testament letters, there is no question that the themes and images of early Christian literature greatly influenced the composition of 1 Clement.

6.3   CONTENTS

Outline of the
Materials

Summary of the
Argument

Greetings to the Corinthians! Our response to your internal conflicts has been delayed by our own problems. But we wish to write now out of respect for your reputation for knowledge, obedience, humility—and unity.

In fact, it is no doubt because of your own good fortune as a growing church that some among you now bring jealousy and disorder to the community. If you will only recall the jealousy of Cain against Abel, Esau against Jacob, Pharaoh against Moses, and other such examples, then you will clearly see your own situation. Remember that in the cases of Peter and Paul, jealousy even resulted in martyrdom. We struggle with these same concerns—and the key is repentance. The history of Israel offers numerous examples of those persons who repented before God, men and women whose obedience, faith, humility, and piety served to save them. For God truly takes notice of those among us who are meek and gentle. Therefore you would do well to follow God's direction, not human impulses. Pursue peace. Seek to be humble like Elijah and Elisha, Job and Moses, and even David before you. And in the same way that all of creation is ordered by its submission to God, so too must you learn submission as a community. Avoid evil and seek what is good and orderly in your lives.

Now be assured that a holy lifestyle will pay rich dividends in the future—through God's promised resurrection. Recall the ancient phoenix who lives its life until death, only then to arise anew. In the same hope let us hold fast to God and the promises of scripture for our lives. In reality, where else can we go? Has God not chosen us to be a holy people? So be the holy people of God in order to have both the privileges and the duties of that promise. As God blessed the patriarchs of Israel, so too will we be blessed if we continue in our good works. We have been patterned in the divine image. God's covenant is upon us. The way of our salvation has come to us through God's own beloved, Jesus Christ, who through his sacrifice of death preserves us to be his living body. And as we are the body of Christ, each part is dependent upon the next.

How then can anyone within the community justify some claim to exalt themselves? They are foolish and ignorant. The Lord has commanded us to offer sacrifices and services in an orderly fashion, and to do otherwise is sin. It is true that there are different functions which must be observed within the structure of the church. Yet these must work together in recognition of the authority for that structure, which has come to us through the apostles, who received it from the Lord Jesus Christ, whose source is God. And the apostles preached that authority in the form of the gospel throughout the empire, so that now we have the elements of priesthood and organization which God has provided for our guidance. You are eager, friends. But remember your scriptures—God rewards those who endure in patience and suffering.

Struggles and schisms among you are intolerable. Paul made this clear to you in his own letters to the community. Do not fall back into a situation of division, but come to some agreement for unity among yourselves. Remember Paul's theme of love, and recall the love which Jesus Christ already showed for you through his death. Your very prayers will reinforce your love. We have all sinned, so be sure to offer forgiveness when necessary. Do not harden yourselves to others with whom you have disagreed in past matters. Confess your sins and, as God reconsidered the fate of the sinful Israelites in the Sinai, so too shall your weaknesses be forgiven. Listen to those who guide you, the presbyters, and submit to their leadership. Has not scripture offered a witness of destruction with respect to those who seek evil and disorder? We pray that God, who is the true power over the creation, may intervene on your behalf.

Now consider what we have said here, and may God bless you. Those who have agreed to bring this letter to you should be sent back quickly so that we may enjoy the good news that you have once again become unified. The Lord's grace be with you.

6.4 RELATED LITERATURE

Barnard, L. W. "St. Clement of Rome and the Persecution of Domitian." In *Studies in the Apostolic Fathers and their Background.* Pages 5–18. New York: Schocken, 1966. (BQ1080.B366 1966)

Bowe, Barbara E. *A Church in Crisis: Ecclesiology and Paraenesis in Clement of Rome.* Philadelphia: Fortress, 1988. (BQ1198.B6 1988)

Brown, Raymond E. and John P. Meier. *Antioch and Rome: New Testament Cradles of Catholic Christianity.* Pages 159–83. New York: Paulist, 1983. (BR165.B67 1983)

Grant, Robert M. and Holt H. Graham. *First and Second Clement.* The Apostolic Fathers 2. New York: Thomas Nelson & Sons, 1965. (BQ1080.A4 1964)

Hagner, Donald A. *The Use of the Old and New Testaments in Clement of Rome.* Supplements to Novum Testamentum 34. Leiden: E. J. Brill, 1973. (BS500.H26 1973)

Hall, S. G. "Repentance in I Clement." In *Studia Patristica.* Edited by F. L. Cross. Volume 8/2, pages 30–43. Texte und Untersuchungen zur Geschichte der altchristlichen Literatur 93. Berlin: Akademie–Verlag, 1966. (BQ26.I5 1963)

Jeffers, James S. *Conflict at Rome: Social Order and Hierarchy in Early Christianity.* Minneapolis: Fortress, 1991. (BR878.R7.J44 1991)

Norris, F. W. "Ignatius, Polycarp and I Clement: Walter Bauer Reconsidered." *Vigiliae Christianae* 30 (1, 1976), pp. 23–44.

Wilhelm–Hooijbergh, A. E. "A Different View of Clemens Romanus." *The Heythrop Journal* 16 (3, 1975), pp. 266–88.

Wong, D. W. F. "Natural and Divine Order in I Clement." *Vigiliae Christianae* 31 (1, 1977), pp. 81–87.

7 The Second Letter of Clement of Rome to the Corinthians (2 Clement)

7.1.1   Manuscript tradition—one complete Greek text; one partial Greek text (1.1–12.5); one Syriac text

7.1.2   Literary form—early Christian homily or sermon (mistakenly called a letter by tradition)

7.1.3   Authorship—unknown Christian (Clement of Rome by tradition, though unlikely)

7.1.4   Date—AD 98–174 (probably AD 120–140)

7.1.5   Setting—unknown (probably either Corinth, Alexandria, or Rome)

7.1.6   Purpose—to support Christian unity against false teachings (perhaps delivered at a service of baptism)

7.1.7   Primary elements—Christology; obedience of the believer; concern for end times

7.1.8   Special images—knowledge of God; immortal contest; potter's clay; neither male nor female; preexistent church

7.1.9   Relationship to scripture—focus on Isaiah; special emphasis on New Testament gospels and writings of Paul

7.2 QUESTIONS

Scholars know of only three copies of the text of 2 Clement. Two of these are written in Greek, the original language of the document. The third text is preserved in Syriac. These three copies of the text appear in the following manuscripts:

7.2.1 Where did we get our text?

(a) Our only complete copy of 2 Clement in Greek may be found in **Codex Hierosolymitanus.** We are already quite familiar with this manuscript as a source for the Letter of Barnabas, our only complete copy of the Didache, the long form of the letters of Ignatius, and 1 Clement. Unfortunately, this document comes from the eleventh century and is rather late in the history of manuscript witnesses. Historians thus find themselves in a situation which has parallels to the case of the Didache: our knowledge of the complete text of 2 Clement in its original Greek language depends primarily on a single, late manuscript. Therefore, there is no solid tradition supporting the text.

(b) The second Greek text appears along with a collection of New Testament writings in **Codex Alexandrinus.** This fifth-century manuscript is widely treasured by historians because it is one of our best witnesses to 1 Clement as well. The fact that 1–2 Clement appear together here suggests that, already by the fifth century, the early church recognized a link between the two writings. Unfortunately, the copy of 2 Clement in **Codex Alexandrinus** is not complete, but extends only through the material in 12.5a. Because this break occurs in mid-sentence, it is impossible to know whether the editor of this **codex** had a complete copy or, perhaps, a form shorter than our present version. Despite the fact that a portion of the original text is missing, the material that does remain is especially important since it is the single means by which scholars can evaluate the form of 2 Clement in **Codex Hierosolymitanus.**

(c) A single Syriac translation of 2 Clement is preserved in a twelfth-century manuscript of biblical writings. Because this copy is a translation and appears in a late manuscript, its value as a witness to the earliest form of the text is limited.

Apart from these three copies of the text, there are no other citations of 2 Clement among the important theologians and historians of the early church. Even **Clement of Alexandria,** who evidences an extensive knowledge of 1 Clement, does not seem to know 2 Clement. Because the text soon became associated with the name of Clement of Rome, especially in the tradition of the Syriac church, it is curious that there is no evidence that the texts of 1–2 Clement circulated together in either the Egyptian (= Coptic) or Western (= Latin) churches. The absence of any copies of 2 Clement in either Coptic or Latin suggests that the text was not widely known or used in those traditions. It is true that a few authors in the Western church do speak of a "second epistle of Clement," but most scholars regard these as referring to another writing, the so-called *Letter of Clement to James* in the literature of the **Pseudo-Clementines.**

Traditionally 2 Clement has been called a letter or epistle. Yet, unlike the letters of 1 Clement and Ignatius, those elements typical of the ancient letter structure—such as a greeting, words of thanksgiving, closing concerns—are absent. Instead, the shape of 2 Clement suggests that the writing was written to serve as a tractate for a specific, early Christian community. It will be recalled that the Letter of Barnabas also was originally written to be delivered in a church setting, though that text ultimately was refashioned into a letter format by a later editor. In many respects the structure of 2 Clement resembles that of Barnabas, though it never assumed the form of a letter and, presumably, was never intended to circulate widely.

Since 2 Clement is therefore not to be considered as a letter, what was its original nature? A scan of the text shows that the author was primarily concerned to instruct Christians about the correct attitude toward God and neighbor during the course of their daily lives. The reader is continually called to live a life of moral righteousness, and the authority of scripture is carefully used to buttress the argument. Furthermore, the author calls for the gathering of the community (17.3) and states quite clearly that the text should be "read aloud" (19.1). These elements strongly suggest that 2 Clement was a homily or sermon designed for a specific occasion. The text thus is quite valuable among ancient Christian writings since it appears to preserve an example of early church preaching.

7.2.2 What form does the text take?

The question of the authorship of 2 Clement has elicted numerous hypotheses and speculations. From the outset, it is generally agreed that the author was not the same individual who wrote 1 Clement. Two basic reasons underlie this assumption—the first derives from the nature of the writing itself; the second comes from a separate historical witness.

In the first instance, there is a distinct contrast in the literary styles of the two texts. This contrast may be explained in some sense by the fact that the writings were composed for separate occasions and to meet different needs. At the same time, however, the marked difference between the vocabulary and syntax of the two works is not so

7.2.3 Who was the author?

easily explained. Such inescapable differences lead scholars to believe it highly improbable that the same author produced both texts.

In the second instance, the early church itself was uncertain about the authorship of the text. Early Christian tradition in Syria attributed various writings to Clement of Rome, as is attested at the conclusion of the late fourth-century *Apostolic Constitutions* (see 8.5.47). Its author lists 1–2 Clement as part of the New Testament **canon** of scriptures. Yet an argument against common authorship had already been raised almost a hundred years previously by the testimony of the early church historian **Eusebius of Caesarea**. At the turn of the fourth century, **Eusebius** insisted that there was no solid historical basis for attributing a second text to Clement of Rome (*Ecclesiastical History* 3.38.4). **Eusebius** is known to have been well-acquainted with numerous ancient manuscripts, and, whenever possible, he sought to associate each text with a specific author (though often in error). Consequently, scholars have typically assumed that **Eusebius** would have gladly attributed the authorship of 2 Clement to Clement of Rome if he could.

Arguments from both style and historical testimony have fairly well discounted any possibility that the author of 1 Clement—whether Clement of Rome or otherwise—was the author of 2 Clement. This means it is necessary to explore some alternatives. Scholars offer three:

(a) An early preacher in Corinth. It is entirely possible that 2 Clement was an ancient homily delivered in the church at Corinth. The author's use of specific imagery in chapter 7, which has been borrowed from athletic competition, is thought by some scholars to have been inspired by Greek sporting events—in particular, the Isthmian games. If the text is traceable to Corinth, this might explain how the homily became associated with the letter of 1 Clement, which itself had been sent to the Corinthian church. For example, the documents may have been stored together in the church's archives, and, with time, both texts became attributed to the author of 1 Clement.

(b) An early preacher in Alexandria. Some scholars argue that it may be best to disregard any external evidence for the authorship of 2 Clement, since such resources are inconclusive. Based upon the textual evidence, they suggest that the homily was originally written in Alexandria, Egypt. The general theological character of 2 Clement certainly recalls typical Alexandrian theology, and the structure of the text is in many respects reminiscent of the Letter of Barnabas, which also is usually associated with Alexandria. On the surface, this

solution does not seem to answer the question of how our text eventually became associated with 1 Clement, which was written in Rome and sent to Corinth. But scholars have long observed that strong associations existed between Alexandria and Rome. There is a distinct possibility that copies of 2 Clement eventually were carried from one city to the other as early Christians traveled between the two regions.

(c) A later preacher in Rome. While the text of 2 Clement may not have come from the hand of Clement around the end of the first century, it could have derived from an unknown preacher in Rome years later. In his *Ecclesiastical History* 4.23.11, **Eusebius** records that the church of Corinth possessed two letters from the church at Rome. The first was associated with Clement and the second with the Roman bishop **Soter** (ca. 166–174). No description of **Soter's** letter is provided by **Eusebius**, but a few scholars think it is possible that this letter incorporated the homily now identified as 2 Clement. Ultimately, if these two writings had been stored together, then the issue of the authorship of 2 Clement might have been forgotten by the time of **Eusebius**. Since both texts were known to have come from Rome, it would have been easy to associate the two writings as letters from Clement.

This brief survey of positions concerning the authorship of 2 Clement does not leave the reader with a clear answer. Each of the explanations offers features deserving consideration, yet the arguments serve better to explain 2 Clement's geographical origins than to resolve the issue of its authorship. As a result, we are left only with the general observation that 2 Clement was composed by an anonymous early Christian preacher.

As with the issue of authorship, the question of a date of composition remains unresolved. Unfortunately, the writing itself contains no references to contemporary events which might offer some key for assigning the text to a specific period of time.

7.2.4 When was the text written?

Most scholars date 2 Clement within a rather broad spectrum of years—the first half of the second century. Those few scholars contending that the writing came from the hand of Clement of Rome traditionally date it several years earlier, to around 98–100. Those attributing the text to **Soter** of Rome propose a date as late as 174. Most scholars find these two solutions to be unacceptable and unnecessarily extreme. It is much more likely that the text arose sometime around the middle of the second century. Two basic arguments are offered in support of this mid-century date:

(a) In 2.4 and 8.5 the author refers to materials from the **synoptic gospels** of the New Testament as *scripture*. This acknowledgment that writings outside of the **canon** of the Old Testament could bear the authority of scripture is not clearly recognized elsewhere among the writings of the apostolic fathers. The texts of the apostolic fathers were generally compiled prior to the widespread efforts of the ancient church to collect the earliest Christian literature for study and use in worship. One should probably assume, therefore, that 2 Clement was composed somewhat later than other documents in the corpus since its author seems fully aware that certain collected writings were beginning to function authoritatively as a **canon** among the churches.

(b) Many scholars assert that 2 Clement was written prior to any threat of **gnosticism** within early Christian churches; thus it came early in the history of Christian literature. Admittedly, there is no specific mention of **gnosticism** within the text. It is difficult to imagine, however, that such a concern does not lie behind our author's message. For example, in 3.1–5 the author is concerned that the reader understand the "true knowledge" of Christ and through him to *know* the Father of truth. This knowledge was not perceived to be a prize for those who possessed it, as was usually preached by the gnostics; rather, it was a motivation to do good works, as is evident from the focus of chapters 4–15. In the same way, the goal of heavenly rest promised by **gnosticism** is redefined in 2 Clement to mean the rest that comes from having done the will of Christ (6.7). The tendency of the author to address such issues strongly suggests that the refutation of **gnosticism** and its theology was a primary concern. Therefore, the text may not be as early as some scholars suggest.

In light of these general considerations, most scholars place 2 Clement between 120 and 140. This time span allows both for the widespread reception of the New Testament writings and for the threat of **gnosticism** among the churches of the Roman Empire. Unfortunately, we lack data to establish a more specific date.

7.2.5 In what setting was the text written?

Specific knowledge about the original setting of the text remains elusive. As a homily, 2 Clement's theme would be applicable for most contexts within early Christianity. Perhaps the most pressing scholarly issue concerns the nature of the recipients. Was 2 Clement originally written primarily for Jewish Christians or non-Jewish Christians?

The overall approach of the text—the call for repentance and good works—may be best understood against the background of contemporary Judaism. The author's decision to focus upon a well-known text from ancient Israel, the Old Testament book of Isaiah, would be an appropriate choice for a homily directed toward a Jewish audience. And, by not having any appeal to the divinity of Jesus Christ, 2 Clement avoids a theological interpretation that would have offended strict Jewish concerns for monotheism—the confession that there is but one true God.

Other scholars argue that the audience was composed primarily to non-Jews. For instance, recipients are twice described as having been "worshipers of idols and dead gods" (1.6–7; 3.1)—a charge typically directed toward the followers of pagan gods. The material between these two passages (see 2.1–7) discusses the call of sinners—those persons who were desolate without God. This probably should be understood as a further reference to the *nations* (non-Jews), those who did not previously possess the promise of God that was offered to the Jews through the Law of Moses. With respect to the divinity of Jesus Christ, the text lacks any specific focus upon this theme, yet the author opens the homily with a call for the audience to "think of Jesus Christ as God" (1.1); the author certainly presumes that this view of Christ should guide the thoughts of the hearer.

Ultimately, there is no conclusive information for determining the nature of the audience of 2 Clement. The author's message of repentance and good works, together with a warning against **gnosticism** and the teachings of **docetism,** need not be restricted to any single geographical location. Indeed, any of the three possible cities of origin suggested above—Corinth, Alexandria, Rome—could have served as a setting for the text.

It is usually acknowledged that 2 Clement was an early homily or sermon. Specifically why this homily was written can be determined to some extent from the author's focus. Three features of the text offer some understanding of this focus:

7.2.6 Why was the text written?

(a) Apparently the text was presented by an individual who had just concluded with a reading of the scriptures within the context of a worship service. Scholars often argue that this conclusion may be deduced from the phrase "I [have just] read to you an appeal to pay attention to what has been written" (19.1). The text's numerous quotations from the book of Isaiah in the Old Testament suggest that in fact the prophecy of Isaiah 54:1 (see 2 Clement 2.1–3) had been read immediately prior to the delivery of the homily. As attested by **Justin Martyr**, the use of the pronoun *I* throughout 2 Clement strongly suggests that many second-century churches came to distinguish between the *reader* and the *preacher* during worship. Our author, on the other hand, appears to have filled both roles. Presumably this person carried some authority as a leader within the early church.

(b) The phrase "pay attention now while we are being warned by the presbyters/elders" (17.3) suggests that the author did not hold the office of presbyter, though this conclusion is not entirely certain. Possibly the speaker was a deacon or someone else of authority within the community. Whatever the case, the author of 2 Clement is concerned that the audience respect the authority of community leaders and rely on them for guidance in the face of daily challenges.

(c) The text's scattered attempts to refute the theological claims of **gnosticism** indicate the author's deliberate effort to combat the threat of hostile forces, possibly within the community itself. The earlier letters of Ignatius and Polycarp show that the rise of **docetism** within the church at the end of the first century was a danger to early Christian communities. This threat, which may already have been the focus of the Gospel of John and much of the apostle Paul's arguments, undoubtedly had become a serious challenge to church leaders by the middle of the second century. Our author seems to have made refuting the challenge of **gnosticism** a primary focus of the homily.

The text of 2 Clement offers a unique blend of elements—a distinct focus on the interpretation of scripture, a specific call to heed the authority of church leaders, and a subtle warning against the promises of false teaching. The combination of these elements suggests that the homily may have been designed to encourage a specific community in its efforts to maintain theological integrity and structural unity. Scholars often observe that this same type of homily would have been equally acceptable during a baptismal service when converts were inducted into the church. Indeed, the author refers to the need of the Christian to keep one's "baptism pure and clean" (6.9) as a symbol of participation in God's kingdom. Elsewhere, the role of baptism as a *seal* for Christian faith becomes a theme for the text (see 7.6; 8.6).

The promise of the Old Testament scriptures, the authority of local church leaders, the threat of false teachers—each of these elements serves as a crucial pillar for the message of the author. Unquestionably this formula also served in one form or another as the basis of Christian homilies and sermons throughout the following centuries.

The structure of 2 Clement suggests a basic division into three primary sections: the first is theological in tone; the second focuses upon the ethical lifestyle; and the third centers upon the final judgment of God. The primary concerns of the author are perhaps best understood in view of these three sections:

7.2.7 What are the primary traits of the text?

(a) Christology. In the first part of 2 Clement (1.1–2.7) the reader encounters the author's foundational assertion about the person of Jesus Christ—he is to be considered "as God, judge of the living and the dead" (1.1). This is not a confession that seeks to associate Jesus and God with respect to identity but, rather, with respect to function. As God bears the ability to save humanity from its sinful state, so too does the agent of God—Christ—receive the same power to achieve human salvation. This salvation has been made available through the suffering that Jesus of Nazareth endured for the sake of the world (1.2), a suffering which demonstrated the mercy of God for those who are perishing.

Specific statements about the nature of Jesus as God's messiah are not offered elsewhere in 2 Clement—except perhaps for the final blessing of 22.5 where the author acknowledges that the savior *was sent* by God as a divine agent. The lack of any general discussion about the nature of Jesus Christ within the homily has led many historians to argue that 2 Clement maintains a low Christology or does not consider that the nature of Jesus as God's agent should be associated with the nature of God in any particular sense. Yet there is some reason to think that this *apparent* lack of christological awareness within the text may not accurately reflect the author's theology. Indeed, 2 Clement presumably has been designed to deflect the speculations of **docetism** that Jesus of Nazareth had not been a true human but had only assumed human form. Such speculations would logically have led to a denial that Jesus could in fact have suffered on the cross—the very premise against which 2 Clement struggles! In this light, it would not have served the author's argument to focus upon the *divine* nature of Jesus.

(b) Obedience of the believer. Echoing a theme typical in much of early Christian literature, section two (3.1–14.5) focuses upon the need of the faithful believer to respond in obedience to the will of Christ. In the view of the author, the foundation for this response is constructed from good works, which are viewed as the reflection of a holy and righteous life. Numerous reflections of the teachings of Jesus as found in the **synoptic gospels** of the New Testament appear in the form of commandments throughout this material: do not follow a desire for material possessions, avoid adultery and corruption, choose to live by pure motives, etc. In response to these teachings, the faithful and obedient disciple of Christ is promised a passage into God's kingdom (11.7).

The structure of this section hinges upon the realization that there are two realities to life—the world of this age and the eternal world of God. In certain ways this teaching is a reflection of the Two Ways motif that already is present in Didache 1–6 and Barnabas 18–20. Those who do not repent and accept the salvation of Christ are viewed as individuals who participate in the present world, the world of material concerns, destructive desires, and death. Obedient followers of Christ, on the other hand, seek to reflect the values of the eternal world of God, to share in the glories of that kingdom, and to gain life. This latter world is both a future reality that is yet to be realized and a present experience that is to be found in the life of the church. It is a world characterized by righteous living and active participation in the power of God's Spirit.

(c) Concern for the end times. The final section of 2 Clement (15.1–20.5) is consumed by the realization that God's judgment is at hand. In certain respects obedient Christians continue to be active in response to this judgment. That response, however, cannot be fulfilled merely through each believer's relationship to their neighbor, but requires that each person turn toward God in prayer (15.3–5). Indeed, in the author's own words, "prayer in good conscience rescues from death" (16.4). The need for prayer is demanded by the times, since those who maintain a holy reverence toward Christ as they seek to follow the *commands of the Lord* will be rescued (17.3). Against the image of this rescue the author offers a portrayal of the horrible torture of eternal damnation in flames (17.7). As a final thought, the hearer is encouraged not to be misled by the unrighteous, who appear to enjoy the riches of the present world. Instead, the reward of the righteous person awaits in the world to come (20.1–4). In this way the judgment of God ultimately rewards those who, like Christ, have suffered for the sake of the gospel.

For such a relatively short piece of early Christian literature, 2 Clement is filled with interesting and unusual images. Some of these appear to draw upon common biblical figures, yet many undoubtedly reveal theological insights that emerged from the author's own reflections. The following themes are worth note:

7.2.8 What special images appear?

(a) Knowledge of God (3.1). The author insists that it is through Christ that humanity has come to *know* the Father of truth, or God. Before **gnosticism** became recognized as a threat to the theological integrity of the developing church in the second century, early Christian literature made free use of the term *knowledge* as a legitimate sign of a life that was in harmony with the will of God. For example, the apostle Paul confirms for the Corinthians that "all Christians possess knowledge" (1 Corinthians 8:1). And in the apostolic fathers, the author of Barnabas writes in order that the reader's "knowledge be made perfect" (1.5), while the author of the Didache gives thanks to God for the "life and knowledge, faith and immortality" which are made known through Jesus (9.3; 10.2).

The author of 2 Clement appears to have moved beyond a naive assumption about the role of knowledge in early Christian thought. The text indicates a greater awareness that there are false teachers who offer a distorted view of knowledge in the belief that some Christians possess this special grace from God, while others do not (10.5). It is not certain who these teachers may have been. **Gnosticism** and gnostic teaching are not condemned specifically, and any of the ancient **mystery religions** of the Mediterranean world may have been in the author's mind. Since the heart of 2 Clement's argument concerns an ethical lifestyle (3.1–14.5), the reader can assume that salvation comes not through any specific, limited knowledge, but only through an obedient response to the sacrifice of Jesus (1.1). Presumably, the author has in mind the threat of **gnosticism** when warnings are made about those persons who teach a false understanding of what it means to possess the knowledge of God.

(b) The immortal contest (7.1–6). The text of 2 Clement draws from the imagery of athletic competition to paint the struggles of Christian living. As mentioned above, many scholars see this as a conscious reflection of the annual games of ancient Greece. If our text originated in Corinth, then the imagery may refer specifically to the traditional Isthmian games conducted in that region. In his correspondence to the Corinthians, the apostle Paul had already observed the need for self-control in order to win the prize for any athletic event (1 Corinthians 9:24–27). The author may be alluding to Paul's language. But 2 Clement adds two interesting observations to this theme: those unable to win the prize can at least strive to come near to it, and those seeking to win a lesser, corruptible prize will be taken aside and punished! In addition, the author portrays the struggle of Christian living as a training ground, a practice session that ultimately leads each faithful athlete to achieve that prize from God which is yet to come (20.2).

(c) The potter's clay (8.1–4). Our author presents an intriguing image of the early Christian as one whose life is being formed by God, much as the clay which a potter shapes into a pot. Undoubtedly, this picture is intended to reflect the Old Testament imagery of Jeremiah 18. In this text God tells the prophet Jeremiah that, as a potter fashions the clay, so too may God form a nation. The peoples of this nation may be used for some divine plan or, if they are defective, may be destroyed in order to be reshaped into a new vessel. As with the athletic imagery in chapter 7, our author once again adds a curious twist. Indeed, a potter can shape the clay only until it is fired in the oven. Afterwards, any spoiled pot must be cast away. In the light of the threat of God's day of fiery judgment (a discussion of which follows in 2 Clement 17.4–7), the call for each reader to become acceptable clay to be shaped by God's hands created a vivid image for the early Christian imagination.

(d) Neither male nor female (12.1–6). In one of the most curious passages of 2 Clement, the author gives a unique interpretation of an early Christian saying. At 12.2 the reader discovers a saying *of the Lord* which reads as follows: the kingdom of the Lord will come "when the two are one, and the outside like the inside, and the male with the female, neither male nor female." Two parallels to this saying occur elsewhere in early Christian literature. One version is known from the *Gospel of the Egyptians,* fragments of which are preserved by **Clement of Alexandria**. But the better parallel comes from the second-century document known as the *Gospel of Thomas* (saying 22.4). Both 2 Clement and the *Gospel of Thomas* offer this peculiar saying as an answer to how one may enter God's kingdom. While the issues are complicated, it seems evident that the version in the **Gospel of Thomas** gives a gnostic interpretation concerning how salvation is obtained by God's chosen people. The text of 2 Clement struggles to avoid any such interpretation of course, and instead applies the teaching to the ethical lifestyle of the Christian believer. For 2 Clement, to see "the male with the female" is to make no distinction between the two genders. When the Christian can achieve this goal in common daily life, then the time for God's kingdom will have arrived.

(e) The preexistent church (14.1–5). In a special plea, the author calls for all Christians to recognize that the church existed in a spiritual form before the creation of the world. As the bride of Christ, the church serves as the residence of God's Spirit. The reader is thus warned: do not abuse the flesh, which is the home of the church, or the Spirit of Christ cannot live there. Already in the Gospel of John in the New Testament there is a clear expression of belief in the preexistent nature of Christ (1.1–5); this undoubtedly reflected common, early speculation about the nature of Jesus of Nazareth. Second Clement's connection between the preexistence of Christ and the church is curious, however. It suggests that second-century Christianity was well on its way toward more specific speculation about the nature of the church, an institution which had come to be seen as the home both of the eternal Christ and of his faithful followers.

7.2.9 How does the text relate to scripture?

There is no question that the author of 2 Clement knows scripture well. On the one hand, the text repeatedly alludes to Old Testament texts, especially the book of Isaiah. At the same time, the author draws upon a wide selection of early Christian writings, especially materials from the **synoptic gospels** and the letters of Paul.

Toward the beginning of the homily the author incorporates materials that undoubtedly were familiar to the audience. These materials are interwoven at 1.4–8 in the form of an early Christian hymn or song. Early hymns, or fragments of hymns, appear occasionally in the New Testament materials—as at Philippians 2:6–11, Hebrews 1:3–13, and John 1:1–18—and were often used as the basis for preaching. In the case of 2 Clement, the hymn in 1.4–8 became a theological foundation for the author's argument as it appeared within the homily. This hymn describes the ignorance and error of those who have not yet come to accept the message of early Christianity. Presumably, it is meant to characterize the Christian community before it came to recognize the importance of the sacrifice of Jesus Christ. This focus is of primary concern to the author, since the effect of the homily depends upon the realization that it was through God's power alone that early Christianity emerged.

Figure 7–A — THE EARLY CHRISTIAN HYMN OF 2 CLEMENT 1.4–8

(v. 4)   For he gave us the light,
    as a father he called us son,
    he saved us while we were perishing.

(v. 6)   We were blinded in our sight,
    worshipping stone and wood and gold and silver and copper—
    the works of humans,
    and our whole life was nothing except death.
    Thus we were covered by darkness and mist filled our eyes,
    though we have received our sight and by his will have cast
    away the cloud which covered us.

(v. 7)   For he pitied us and saved us,
    seeing the great error and destruction in us
    and that we had no hope of salvation except through him.

(v. 8)   For he called us before we came to be,
    and he desired that we should come to exist out of nothing.

The homily next turns to Isaiah 54:1—"Sing O barren one who did not bear; burst into song and shout, you who have not been in labor! For the children of the desolate woman will be more than the children of her that is married." Our author here clearly equates the *barren woman* with the institution of the church, which did not bear fruit until God provided her with children. In this respect the audience is called to recognize that Christian faith has the witness of the ancient Jewish prophets. The words of Isaiah are woven throughout the text to support the author's arguments, though only scattered references to the book appear elsewhere (see 3.5; 7.6; 13.2; 17.4–5). Because the prophecy of Isaiah serves as the guiding principle for the homily's message, scholars generally believe that 2 Clement was designed to comment on a portion of Isaiah 54 read during a service of worship.

While the primary theme of 2 Clement has been derived from the author's reading of Isaiah, the support for that message is borrowed from literature produced by the early Christian community. One rather obvious source for this material is found in the **synoptic**

gospels. Of these three gospels, the text of 2 Clement appears to employ numerous sayings from the Gospels of Matthew and Luke, but only a few from the Gospel of Mark. In most cases the sayings are directed toward some aspect of Jesus' role and function as God's messiah. Their purpose is to assist in defining Jesus Christ for Christian faith, rather than clarifying the nature of Jesus' message during his ministry. While many texts in the apostolic fathers use similar sayings that circulated in an oral form prior to their incorporation into the New Testament gospels, the sayings of 2 Clement appear to have been taken directly from the gospel literature. The fact that our author seems to have been aware of several of these gospels further supports a later date of composition.

A second important source in 2 Clement is the letters of Paul. While our author does not refer to Paul by name, typical Pauline images appear throughout the writing. For example, Isaiah 54:1, quoted in 2.1 as the focus of the homily message, is also quoted by Paul in Galatians 4:27. In this particular instance, it is likely that our author is not borrowing from Galatians but directly from Isaiah, since Paul's argument leads to the view that Christians are a free people, while no mention of freedom in Christ arises in 2 Clement. At the same time, it is curious that both Paul and the author of 2 Clement associate the *barren woman* of Isaiah with the church.

Other specific images and illusions in the homily recall the writings of Paul. The first is the image of the potter and the clay at 8.1–3. As observed above, our author presumably borrows this image from Jeremiah 18. Yet, once again, Paul himself makes a similar allusion in Romans 9:19–24. Additional parallels may derive from Paul's correspondence with the Corinthians. Recall the plea in 2 Clement 7.1–6 that each Christian compete as an athlete of God; this seems to reflect Paul's imagery in 1 Corinthians 9:24–27. So too, our author's warning in 3.1 not to worship or make sacrifices to dead gods probably should be read against Paul's own command in 1 Corinthians 8:1. And finally, 2 Clement's association between the human body as the church into which Christ has come bears interesting parallels to Paul's insistence that the body is the temple of Christ in 1 Corinthians 6:12–20. Such imagery strongly suggests that our author had an extensive knowledge of Paul's theology, and probably had access to some form of 1 Corinthians.

Outline of the Materials

Summary of the Argument

We must come to recognize Jesus Christ as our eternal judge, as we have with God, for what Christ has done for us is no trivial matter. Though we were nothing, he endured a great suffering for us. We are compelled, therefore, to rejoice in the salvation he has provided.

Christ's mercy toward us demands that we respond. No longer can we worship dead gods, but we must honor Christ in word and deed. We must be aware that this world is but a temporary place and that its charms are false. Our home is with the future kingdom of God. So we must run a good and faithful race toward that goal. Now is the time to repent of our worldly desires—to keep ourselves pure in order to honor our baptism. It is our very flesh which will be raised at the salvation of the faithful. So let us not be tempted by the pleasures of the flesh, but let us be pure in our desires. Do not be indecisive! Wait for God's kingdom. And remember that the attitude of your soul can be judged by the actions which you do and the way in which you treat one another. Indeed, when we can all finally learn to see each other as equals, then God's kingdom will come. Let us repent and learn to honor the needs of others, and not simply our own needs. For such is the nature of Christ's living body, the church, which was created in spirit before the heavens were formed and which now dwells in the flesh of those who honor the Lord. This is our gift of life through the Holy Spirit.

Let us be righteous, holy, and full of prayer in order to secure our salvation. For God has made us a promise, and the day of our judgment quickly approaches. Let us be gracious to others, fast continually, love freely, and remember that prayer saves us from death. If we will only repent of our desires, then the Lord will gather us together at the time of judgment. The righteous will be rewarded; the sinners will be destroyed. I admit that I too am sinful and subject to temptations. Yet scripture promises that if we seek to do righteousness, then we shall ultimately be saved. Do not be misled by the apparent wealth of those unrighteous people who are around you, for your reward will be greater still. Glory be to the immortal God.

7.4 RELATED LITERATURE

Bartlett, Vernon. "The Origin and Date of 2 Clement." *Zeitschrift für neutestamentliche Wissenschaft* 7 (2, 1906), pp. 123–35.

Bornkamm, Günther. "The History of the Origin of the So-Called Second Letter to the Corinthians." In *The Authorship and Integrity of the New Testament.* Edited by Kurt Aland and others. Pages 73–81. S.P.C.K. Theological Collections 4. London: S.P.C.K., 1965. (BS2393.A78 1965)

Chavasse, Claude. *The Bride of Christ: An Enquiry into the Nuptial Element in Early Christianity.* London: Faber & Faber, 1940. (BT205.C48 1940)

Crafer, T. W. *Second Epistle of Clement to the Corinthians.* London: S.P.C.K., 1921. (BR65.C55.S4 1921)

Donfried, Karl Paul. *The Setting of Second Clement in Early Christianity.* Supplements to Novum Testamentum 38. Leiden: E. J. Brill, 1974. (BQ1196.C7.D6 1974)

———. "The Theology of 2 Clement." *Harvard Theological Review* 66 (4, 1973), pp. 487–501.

Grant, Robert M. and Holt H. Graham. *First and Second Clement.* The Apostolic Fathers 2. New York: Thomas Nelson & Sons, 1965. (BQ1080.A4 1964)

Harris, J. Rendel. "The Authorship of the So-Called Second Epistle of Clement." *Zeitschrift für neutestamentliche Wissenschaft* 23 (3, 1924), pp. 193–200.

Koester, Helmut. *Introduction to the New Testament.* Volume 2, pages 233–36. Philadelphia: Fortress, 1982. (BS2410.K613 1982)

Streeter, B. H. *The Primitive Church Studied with Special Reference to the Origins of the Christian Ministry.* Pages 238–55. London: Macmillan, 1930. (BR165.S8 1930)

8 The Shepherd of Hermas

8.1.1 Manuscript tradition—three Greek texts (incomplete); two Latin texts; one Ethiopian text; numerous fragments in Greek, Coptic, and Middle Persian; quotations in Clement of Alexandria and later authors

8.1.2 Literary form—apocalypse formed from a series of visions, a Jewish-Christian homily, and a collection of ancient parables

8.1.3 Authorship—unknown Christian (possibly a contemporary of Pope Pius I)

8.1.4 Date—ca. AD 90–100 (chapters 1–24); ca. AD 100–154 (chapters 25–114)

8.1.5 Setting—Rome, during times of persecution and internal divisions

8.1.6 Purpose—to recall a satisfied church to a pure faith and correct ethical lifestyle

8.1.7 Primary elements—penance; inconsistent Christology; traits of the Holy Spirit

8.1.8 Special images—*Book of Eldad and Modat*; the tower, the virtues; the Leviathan; marriage, adultery, and remarriage; sensual nature of the spirit

8.1.9 Relationship to scripture—no specific use of either the Old or New Testaments

8.2 QUESTIONS

8.2.1 Where did we get our text?

The text of the Shepherd is conserved for us in several ancient manuscripts and in numerous scattered fragments. Unfortunately, none of these sources contains all of the materials which today have been reconstructed into the 114 chapters of the text. Versions of the Shepherd appear in a variety of languages, including Greek—the original language of the text—Latin, Coptic, Ethiopic, and Middle Persian. The Shepherd is preserved in the following manuscripts:

(a) Our oldest copy of the Shepherd appears in **Codex Sinaiticus**. Discovered in 1844 at St. Catherine's Monastery on Mount Sinai, this fourth-century **codex** is an important witness to the development of both the Old and New Testaments, as well as to the Letter of Barnabas. With respect to the text of the Shepherd, only 1.1–31.6 is preserved. Though the **Codex Sinaiticus** is the oldest of the manuscript versions, its abbreviated form of the Shepherd severely limits its usefulness for the purpose of reconstruction.

(b) The fourteenth/fifteenth-century manuscript known as Codex Athous contains the most complete version of the Shepherd in Greek. The majority of this **codex** may be found in the library at the Monastery of Hagios Gregorios on Mount Athos in Greece, though several portions are housed in the library at the University of Leipzig. One page of the text has been lost. Included in the **codex** is the bulk of the text (1.1–107.2), with the omission of only the final portion of the last two parables (107.3–114.5). While this manuscript preserves the materials in their original Greek, its value as a source is often debated because of the late date of the **codex** and the long history of transmission behind the text.

(c) The University of Michigan is home to a third form of the Greek text known as Papyrus 129. This third-century manuscript contains 51.8–82.1, or most of the Parables. Curiously, the text of the Shepherd has been preserved here on the back of an older documentary text.

(d) Two versions of the text are preserved in Latin translations. The first version circulated as a form of the **Vulgate** text and was originally published in Paris. This manuscript is an important tool for reconstructing 107.3–114.5 since the majority of the Greek text for these materials is now lost. The second, and less important, Latin version appears in the so-called Palatine text from the fifteenth century. This manuscript, currently housed in the Vatican Library of Rome, allows scholars to evaluate the translation of the **Vulgate** text against a second Latin translation.

(e) There is a single translation of the text in Ethiopic. Unfortunately, this version provides little new help for understanding the manuscript tradition.

(f) In addition to these manuscripts numerous fragments exist in Greek and Middle Persian, as well as in Coptic—both in the Sahidic and Achmimic dialects; these now are scattered among numerous libraries and private collections. While such fragments offer some limited help in reconstructing the original Greek text, especially the final chapters, their contribution is not otherwise significant.

(g) Short quotations from the Shepherd appear in the writings of **Clement of Alexandria** from the beginning of the third century, as well as in a few other later Christian writings. These references are scattered and incomplete, however, and are of little help to scholars.

8.2.2 What form does the text take?

Scholars usually consider the text of the Shepherd to be an early example of Christian **apocalyptic literature.** The primary purpose of **apocalyptic literature** was to reveal hidden truths to its readers. These truths could take various forms, depending upon the message which the author wished to emphasize, but typically they included explanations about the work of God in recent historical events and the nature of God's activity in the future. Other examples of such literature include the text of Daniel in the Old Testament and Revelation in the New Testament. Outside of scripture, **apocalyptic literature** was widely produced by Jewish authors until the end of the first century AD. Christian authors wrote similar texts during the first and second centuries.

The structure of the Shepherd may be divided according to two systems of understanding. The first system was imposed by the author, or perhaps by some early editor of the text. This view distinguishes three divisions among the materials—the Visions, the Commandments (or Mandates), and the Parables (or Similitudes). Within these three primary sections, the author divides the text into five Visions, twelve Commandments, and ten Parables in order to provide a general structure to the materials. The reason for these divisions in not clear, but it is quite likely that many portions of the text were borrowed from separate sources and were collected into this form in order to create an intelligible narrative.

A second system for interpreting the text has been imposed by modern scholars. This approach seeks to determine how the various portions of the writing are related as literature, with less concern about the author's divisions. For example, there is a difference between the last of the five Visions and the previous four. In the

Greek text, the first four Visions are named, numbered, and specifically called *visions*. Each is devoted to the appearance of the church as a woman who reveals specific information to the author. The fifth Vision, however, is instead called an *apocalypse*. This material introduces the reader to the angel of repentance who takes the form of a shepherd. It is from the revelations of this shepherd (and hence the name of the text) that the Commandments and Parables are then offered.

The modern system of interpretation divides the text into 114 chapters. This division does not require that the Shepherd be distinguished as three main parts, but permits the many segments of the text to stand separately. The discussion below follows the modern division of the Shepherd into chapters. (The text is divided both according to the traditional system and the modern system in the *Outline of the Materials* on page 154)

The manuscript evidence offers some reason to think that the first four Visions circulated separately until they were combined with the fifth by an editor. In certain respects, these four Visions are unrelated to the form and much of the content of the remaining materials. A secondary combination of the materials also explains literary problems associated with the flow of the writing.

There is further reason to think that the Commandments and Parables originally derived from separate sources. Certain scholars note, for example, that the Commandments are offered in the typical style of an ancient Jewish-Christian homily, which may suggest that they were composed as a single literary unit. At the same time, the Parables draw from numerous images occurring throughout ancient literature, and may themselves represent the combination of different sources prior to their inclusion into the Shepherd. As is easily seen, attempts to explain the sources behind the text and how these sources were brought together are complicated and problematic.

8.2.3 Who was the author?

Little can be known with certainty about the author of the Shepherd. If one can assume that the introductory information about the narrator may be applied to the author as well—and is not simply included as the details of a good story—then the following observations apply. Prior to the composition of the text, the author was a slave named Hermas (1.5) who had been sold to the woman Rhoda, presumably a wealthy citizen in Rome (1.1). She, in turn, gave him his freedom. By the time the Shepherd was written, Hermas had become a merchant; he was married and had several children. In addition, one receives the impression over the course of the Shepherd that Hermas himself is a Christian. It is soon revealed to Hermas in a vision that his family life does not fit the mold of the ideal Christian family. His children have "sinned against the Lord" (3.1) and his wife talks too much (6.3). This in itself is not to say that Hermas is unhappy with his family, however. The only clue that he might in any way be dissatisfied is revealed when he sees Rhoda bathing in the river years after he had been given his freedom. In his heart, Hermas says to himself: "I should be happy to have a wife of such beauty and manner" (1.2). With regard to his children, the reader is told that it is precisely because Hermas has failed to correct his children that they have sinned. Otherwise, there is no reason to think that Hermas has any distinguishing characteristics.

Several other attempts have been made to define more specifically who our author may have been. The primary suggestions fall into two basic types, depending on (1) whether the text was written by a single individual, or (2) is instead the product of several contributors. Arguments for a single author include the following proposals:

(1) Single-author auguments

(a) A few scholars suggest that the author of the Shepherd was actually the apostle Paul. This argument is based upon the New Testament text of Acts 14:12, which records that the people of the city of Lystra (in Asia Minor) referred to Paul as the Greek god Hermes, because he was such a profound messenger. This explanation is not widely accepted.

(b) The apostle Paul himself refers to a certain Hermas when he writes to the community at Rome (see Romans 16:14). The early third-century theologian **Origen** in Alexandria, as well as **Jerome** years later, argued that this Hermas was the author of the Shepherd. The value of this suggestion is that it affords an apostolic basis for the work.

(c) The **Muratorian canon,** a list of New Testament writings thought to have been authoritative within the early church, refers to Hermas as the brother of **Pius** (= Pope **Pius I**), the bishop of Rome (ca. AD 140–154). This is perhaps as late as the text could have been composed, since **Irenaeus** also refers to the text in his own work a few decades later (ca. 175). It is strange that the text of the Shepherd reveals no particular awareness of **Pius** in his role as bishop (see 8.3), yet the tradition appears to be quite ancient. Some scholars think that the witness of the **Muratorian canon** reveals the confusion of the early Christian tradition about the authorship of the Shepherd. For example, it may be that the text was written over a number of years and only reached its final form during the time of **Pius**. In either case, the **Muratorian canon** usually receives special consideration by scholars as a witness to the authorship of the Shepherd.

(d) In the second vision (8.3), Hermas is instructed to send a little book of information to a certain Clement so that he might send it "to the cities abroad." Some scholars insist that this Clement was the author of 1 Clement, and thus that our Hermas was his contemporary.

(2) Multiple-author auguments

Other arguments contend that there was more than one author. If any of these explanations can be trusted, then the writing's association with the name *Hermas* has no particular use as far as identifying the actual author. Most proposals for multiple authorship focus upon the different forms in the text: Visions, Commandments, and Parables. It is entirely possible that each of these sections was created by a different author, whose works were then combined by yet another person. Such explanations typically do not distinguish between *authors* and *sources*. Thus it is difficult to state specifically where one author ends and another begins. Arguments trying to distinguish between divergent theological perspectives in the Shepherd usually ignore the question of sources.

A careful analysis of the Shepherd reveals a consistent use of vocabulary and style. In addition, a certain thematic unity binds the writing in its current form. These elements would appear to argue for a single author behind the work. It is more likely, however, that this person was a final editor who combined materials from several sources, making significant alterations in order to provide some theological consistency to the materials.

The document seems to have taken its final shape in stages over an extended period of time, perhaps beginning by the end of the first century and concluding toward the middle of the second century. If one can accept the testimony of the **Muratorian canon** with respect to authorship, then the mid-second century dates of **Pius I** must be the latest possible time of composition.

8.2.4 When was the text written?

Presumably, during this period the sources behind the text were drawn into a single document. It is possible that the instruction to Hermas that he write "two little books" (see 8.3) indicates that the author originally planned to work on separate texts (now combined into our present writing) that reflected revelations and teachings that arose over the course of many years. This time frame may easily have stretched back to the years of Clement of Rome at the end of the first century.

Specific elements in the text support attempts to date the text in this way. These elements may be categorized individually:

(a) Chapters 1–24 (= Visions 1–4) show indications of the situation of the early church. For example, as is indicated by 6.7, some form of persecution of the church is soon to come—or, if viewed in hindsight by the author, has recently occurred. Early Christianity suffered specific persecutions under the rule of the emperors **Nero** (54–68) and **Domitian** (81–96). It may be that the author refers to one of these occasions. The images associated with this persecution resemble those in the late first-century book of Revelation in the New Testament, such as the fact that Rome is equated with *the beast* (see Shepherd 22.6–9). Ultimately, however, the anticipated threat in the Shepherd does not bring harm to the community in Rome itself.

As further testimony to the early nature of these chapters, the author envisions a primitive understanding of church offices. For example, the author continues to be influenced by the role of the New Testament apostles. As paralleled in the writings of Ignatius of Antioch, the role of *apostle* remains as an office in the early church community (13.1), together with that of bishop, teacher, and deacon. In addition, the author does not clearly distinguish among the rulers of the church—calling them both *presbyters* and *bishops*. The evidence indicates that there is no firm understanding of two distinct offices. This suggests that the leadership of the community consisted of several individuals and did not depend on a single bishop (see 8.3; 13.1).

The argument from literary imagery and church structure suggest that the author wrote during the general period of Clement of Rome at the end of the first century (see 8.3).

(b) Chapters 25–114 (= Vision 5–Parables 10) show signs of a later composition. In 92.4 (= Parable 9) the period of the apostles is finished and is now viewed with respect and reverence. The church is faced with the problem of wavering Christians who have lost faith in the face of adversity. There is a call to reject those for whom there no longer appears to be any hope (see 94.3–4). False believers and blasphemers seem to have arisen after the time of persecutions (see 72.4; 74.2). These have no hope for repentance.

Chapters 1–24 and 25–114 appear to form a natural division; perhaps another argument for different periods of composition. Each section's concerns and assumptions reflect a developing church situation. Chapters 1–24 indicate a community in the immediate crisis of some external threat, an immature congregation with a flawed view of the church. Chapters 25–114, on the other hand, come from an established community confronted by an internal threat—the challenge of members who have fallen out of favor through their actions and beliefs. The first section may be easily assigned to the second half of the first century, perhaps between the reigns of **Nero** and **Domitian** (roughly AD 55–100). Because of the mention of Clement in 8.3, possibly a reference to Clement of Rome (bishop ca. AD 88–97), the last decade of the century may be preferred. The second section may fall anywhere within the first half of the second century, though certainly by the time of **Pius I** (ca. 150).

Scholars agree that the text of the Shepherd was written in or near the city of Rome and was intended to address the Christian church there. As with the date of composition, the setting would seem to suggest at least two phases in the development of the church at Rome. Three elements deserve consideration here:

8.2.5 In what setting was the text written?

(a) The sources behind the text. There is little question that the present form of the Shepherd was shaped by numerous source materials. These almost certainly include certain Parables in chapters 50–114, such as the parable of the two cities (chapter 50) and the parable of the vine and the elm (chapter 51). It is quite likely that the general construction of the Commandments in chapters 25–49 was formed with the use of an early homily, perhaps delivered at a service of worship in Rome. The nature of these source materials frustrates any attempt to determine an original setting. This is particularly true in light of the general nature of the images, which could be either from a Jewish background or from some Greek heritage. In either case, they are in no sense specifically Christian in their perspective.

(b) Chapters 1–24. As noted above, these materials are concerned with some outside threat facing the church at Rome. Although the author anticipated that this challenge to the church was yet to come, it is certainly possible that the community was already experiencing the trials described here. The persecutions of the church under the reigns of **Nero** and **Domitian** offer sufficient evidence to suggest that these chapters describe the horrors which the early Christians of Rome experienced as the church emerged at the center of the Roman Empire.

(c) Chapters 25–114. These materials present a different perspective on the life of the church at Rome. By the time of this source's composition the congregation was no longer experiencing the immediate threat of an outside persecution but, instead, had become satisfied with its status and growth. The new problem was the threat of schism. These chapters propose two arguments concerning how the church could shape its lifestyle. In the Commandments, the reader encounters a call to keep to the basic values of God's ethical demands for humanity—be simple and innocent, love truth, maintain purity, have faith, and revere God. The Parables offer concrete images of how the community must establish relationships among its members. The rich are to assist the poor. All Christians are to live for a future, better world, and not for the present, evil age. Each believer is to attend to his or her own faith. This concern for the inner life of the community strongly suggests that the congregation has matured. Unlike that church of an earlier age that required support in the face of adversity, the church is now called to examine herself and to become reformed into the community of believers which Christ desires.

8.2.6 Why was the text written?

The question of why the Shepherd was written can be answered only from the perspective of the final date of composition. The imagery of chapters 1–24 suggests a period of persecution within the church. There is little doubt that the author writes to encourage faithful Christians in the face of their trials and sufferings. The imagery of chapters 25–114 suggests that a period of complacency has come upon the community and that a new prophetic challenge must be offered to its members. Presumably, the message of the first section (chapters 1–24) is intended to serve as a prelude to the message of the second section (chapters 25–114) since the latter text reflects the more recent situation of the church to which the author writes. One may assume that the audience is asked to recall the history of its own persecutions and the grace of God which rescued it from that fate. This would serve as a strong reason for the audience to listen to the prophetic call to reexamine itself in light of its newfound prosperity.

If the text of the Shepherd can be assigned to Rome and attributed to an author associated with that church's leadership, then an important question must be raised. Is the author addressing the failings of the community in general or, instead, is the author more concerned to correct specific abuses within the church's leadership? Some scholars suggest that the Shepherd represents a movement within the church at Rome to reform the community. This reform would have attempted to bring harmony to a divided congregation that had separated the concerns of the wealthy from the needs of the underprivileged.

The Shepherd was widely used throughout the early church and until the time of **Origen** was generally recognized as bearing the authority of scripture. Its two primary themes—awareness of both the threat of outside persecution and the threat of internal dissension—would have had an immediate, practical appeal to early Christianity's churches. In its final form, as can be determined by the themes of chapters 25–114, the prophecy of the Shepherd is directed to those in control of the church. These themes are related to faith and wealth: faith must be lived in humble obedience, not in pompous splendor; wealthy Christians must share their possessions with the poor; the future of the church is built upon the faith and suffering of its past apostles. Finally, according to the instructions of the woman/church who revealed herself to Hermas, these words are to be directed not to the community in general but to "the elders who are in charge of the church" (8.3).

Hermas had been charged to write two books. One copy was to be sent to all the churches, while the other was to be read in "this city"—Rome. Though Hermas himself does not appear to have carried the authority of an official leader in the community, the message of the Shepherd bears the authority of divine revelation. It was the eternal church herself who came to Hermas in the beginning with the message that only the pure in faith would be considered as a valid part of the Christian community. Thereafter, it was the angel of repentance in the form of a shepherd who declared how satisfied Christians must renew their faith in God and redirect their relationships with others. The difficulty for the community was no longer that its existence was threatened, but that it was developing into a new institution whose relationship to Christ was no longer valid.

The shape of the Shepherd's final form in the middle of the second century reveals several key themes. Each of these appears as part of a larger message concerned with the revitalization of the church. It may be useful to review these different themes with this larger concern in mind, especially as it reflects the Shepherd's concern for the appropriate lifestyle of the early Christian.

(a) Penance. Perhaps the one theme most widely associated with the Shepherd is that of penance. It seems that the early church in Rome taught that, having once been baptized, any Christian who sinned after that could not receive further forgiveness from God. The author insists that further forgiveness is indeed possible—but only once! This message is clearly stated in four different passages—6.4; 29.8; 49.2; and 77.1–5. The key to this interpretation of forgiveness in the mind of the author is that the sinner must repent in good faith and, thereafter, must make an honest effort to live a consistent life of obedience.

It should come as no surprise that the topic of repentance is so central. In each of the five Visions there is a focus on Hermas's own need to repent. In the last of these Visions, Hermas is confronted by the shepherd after whom the text has been named, and the shepherd is revealed to be the *angel of repentance*. Yet the author is not concerned simply with the topic of *repentance*. The author is interested primarily in *penance,* that is, repentance by those who already had repented, been baptized into the church of Christ, and subsequently had fallen away. The long parable of the willow tree in chapters 67–77 (= Parable 8) is devoted exclusively to this theme. Here the author stresses the different types of Christians who have been called in faith and yet have lost their devotion to obedience. The use of many categories of people illustrates that the author did not consider the issue of repentance, or penance, to be a simple matter. The question of judgment and forgiveness remains to be decided by God alone. Nevertheless, the author insists that forgiveness is possible for those who have sinned after baptism—though a new commitment to a lifestyle of obedience to God is required.

(b) Inconsistent Christology. The text of the Shepherd does not reveal a consistent understanding of Christology. For instance, in 6.8

the author declares that "the Lord has sworn through his son" that
those who deny Christ will be rejected. But the focus here is less
upon the work of Christ than upon the intentions of God. Subsequent images of Christ as the keeper of God's vineyard (chapters
58–59) and as the essence of God's message to humanity (69.2; 77.1)
also say less about Christ than about the activity of God.

Only in chapters 78–110 (= Parable 9) does the image of Christ
receive any extensive development. Each item of the parable must be
understood according to the **allegorical method** of interpretation,
because each of the parable's images offers a specific meaning. The
essential structure of the parable describes a rock in which there is a
door. Upon this rock there is a tower being built. Quickly the reader
discovers that the rock is Christ, and that the tower is the church,
which has been fashioned upon this solid foundation. This same
Christ—the Son of God—is *older than the creation* itself, though he
has been made new in Jesus of Nazareth (= the door in the rock) so
that believers may enter into God's kingdom. The purpose of the
parable is to lead Hermas to understand that only those who seek
God's kingdom in purity and faith can be admitted. The shepherd
insists that the mercy of Christ is sufficient for this task, though it
should not be abused.

It may be tempting to see a reflection of Christ in the figure of
the shepherd (first appearing to Hermas in chapter 25 = Vision 5).
This association is suggested at first glance by the shepherd's role as
one who reveals the commandments of God to Hermas. This recalls
how the early church interpreted Christ as the one who revealed the
gospel to humanity. There is no real justification for this association,
however. In fact, the author of the Shepherd specifically identifies
the shepherd as an *angel*, and in many respects the shepherd serves
in the role of Hermas's *guardian angel*.

It is quite possible that the Shepherd's inconsistent christological themes and images may reflect the use of different sources
throughout the text. In either case, the author does not show any
particular desire to focus upon the life and ministry of Jesus of
Nazareth or upon the significance of the gospel message with respect
to the daily lifestyle of the Christian community at Rome.

(c) Traits of the spirit. Throughout the Shepherd there is a clear
thread of concern for the work of God's spirit within the church.
This is especially true in the revelation of the shepherd—both within
the Commandments and the Parables. In the Commandments the
spirit is characterized in several ways. First, the spirit which guides

the Christian conscience is a "spirit of truth" (28.4). This emphasis upon conscience and truth is broadly reflected in early Christian theology. In Matthew 5:23 the reader is counseled to make peace with any person whom she or he may have offended before any sacrifice can be made to God. So too, Hebrews 10:22 insists that Christians approach God with a clean conscience. In the apostolic fathers, a similar concern for a clean and pure conscience at the time of prayer is demanded by Didache 4.14 and Barnabas 19.2, a motif which each text presumably borrowed from a common source. Hermas himself is challenged by the shepherd as someone who lives with an *evil* conscience because his sins have not been forgiven. This is revealed to him through the spirit of God.

Second, the spirit of God is *delicate* and *gentle* and is easily choked by an evil spirit (33.2–4; 34.5–7). The author continually emphasizes that evil actions and wicked intentions are a deterrent to the presence of the spirit in the life of the Christian. This produces a struggle between the virtue of patience and the vice of ill temper. The shepherd insists that ill temper and impatience are marks of those persons in whom the spirit of God does not dwell—nor can it thrive in such people. One must assume that an ill-tempered mind-set was viewed by the author of the Shepherd as a common characteristic of those who had fallen away from the teachings of the church.

Finally, human *grief* is a deterrent to the presence of the spirit. The author makes this the primary focus of the argument in chapters 40–42 (= Commandment 10). This theme, while not broadly encountered in scripture (see Isaiah 63:10; Ephesians 4:30), did arise when Christians were persecuted either by Judaism or by the Roman Empire. The role of grief and the threat of a loss of faith ultimately led to divisions between those who remained strong participants within the church during persecution and those who felt the need to abandon Christianity. In this respect, Hermas is informed by the shepherd that grief *wears out* the spirit and that the believer must be cheerful and positive in all aspects of life.

The author then continues with an understanding of the spirit of God in the Parables, specifically in Parables 5 (= chapters 54–60) and 9 (= chapters 78–110). Here the reader discovers that *the holy spirit has existed before creation,* even as the church itself has. The author's position is not exactly clear with respect to the distinction between the *son* of God and the *spirit* of God in this discussion. For example, in Parable 5 certain manuscripts of the Shepherd identify the son with the spirit specifically, though other manuscripts avoid this connection. On the one hand, this problem exists because of the history of manuscript transmission. At the same time, however, it is probable that the author—most likely in reflection of the thought of the community at Rome—wrote prior to a time when a clear distinction between *son* and *spirit* had been formulated for the early Christian community. In other words, the theological doctrine that God is *three-in-one* (Father—Son—Holy Spirit) had not yet been firmly established for our author. With respect to Parable 5, the spirit is associated with God much as the son of God is associated with God. This connection in the Shepherd is similar to that of Jesus Christ and the Paraclete as portrayed in the Gospel of John in the New Testament. These associations indicate the significance that early Christian authors held for the role of the spirit in the life and theology of the church.

In Parable 9 the spirit of God is identified in two distinct forms. Hermas is told at the beginning of the parable (78.1) that the spirit previously had spoken with him *in the form of the church.* Furthermore, that spirit is equated with *the son of God.* As in the case of Parable 5 above, the son is associated here with the spirit. Yet, the reader also discovers that the church stands as the vessel in which the spirit resides. The visions that Hermas is permitted to see throughout the Shepherd are made possible by the spirit through the revelation of the church as a woman. This is indeed curious, since the reader now comes to understand that it is the spirit who gives Hermas the strength to receive these visions and provides the visions themselves. The author seems to have viewed the work of the spirit both as preparation for the receipt of revelation and as a vehicle by which revelation could occur.

The spirit is revealed in this parable in yet a second set of images. Twelve virgins stand around the rock upon which the church (as a tower) is constructed. Hermas learns that these young women bear the names of Christian virtues, yet at the same time they are manifestations of the spirit. The virgins are depicted as young, strong women who are prepared for service to God. Indeed, they assist in the movement of stones for the construction of the tower (= church). Once again, the role of the spirit seems to have been all-pervasive for the author, since we now find an image of the church—as filled with the spirit—under construction with the assistance of the spirit itself. There is some consistency in the imagery since as church and as virgins the church is depicted in the form of women. Earlier comments in the Commandments about the *delicate* nature of the spirit seem to reinforce this feminine connotation of the spirit within the mind of the author.

8.2.8 What special images appear?	With its collection of Visions, Commandments, and Parables, the Shepherd contains intriguing images from the early Christian imagination. These are often quite diverse and sometimes reveal a certain inconsistency in presentation.

(a) *Book of Eldad and Modat*. While scholars now believe that the author of the Shepherd drew on numerous sources in the compilation of the text, only a single source has been acknowledged—the *Book of Eldad and Modat* (see 7.4). The figures of Eldad and Modat are mentioned in the Old Testament at Numbers 11:26 (here as Eldad and Medad), where they are recorded to have been two Israelite prophets who prophesied without the official approval of Moses. The book of prophecy associated with these names apparently was widely known in early Christian circles, though specific references to the work are scattered and few. Apart from its quotation here, some scholars think this lost book may have been a source for 1 Clement 23.3–4 as well as for 2 Clement 2.2–4 and 11.2. It is mentioned as well by the fourth-century author **Epiphanius** of Salamis.

(b) The tower (chapters 10–17, 78–110). The image of the church as a tower is found in two separate sequences of materials. Chapters 10–17 form part of Vision 3, which the church, here in the form of a woman, revealed to Hermas. The tower is being built upon the water with square stones; these are being brought by thousands of workers from the depths of the ocean and from the surrounding lands. Seven women support this tower as it is built. Six young men are responsible for constructing the tower; the men have carefully selected and used many stones, but they have also rejected many others. The woman explains that the tower is in fact herself—the church—which is being built upon the water because salvation comes through water. One presumes that this is a reference to early Christian baptism. The builders of this structure are the holy angels of God; the women are the virtues of Christian living. The stones themselves represent apostles, bishops, teachers, and deacons (some of whom have died since the construction of the tower was begun) and other faithful members of the church. The rejected stones symbolize persons with no faith or whose sins have made them unacceptable.

Figure 8-A — THE VISIONS OF THE TOWER: SHEPHERD 10–17, 78–110

Chapters 10–17	Meaning of the Images
1. tower	church
2. built on the water	salvation through baptism
3. built by six young men	chief holy angels of God
4. thousands of helpers	other holy angels of God
5. supported by seven women	virtues of Christian living
6. four square base stones	apostles, bishops, teachers, deacons
7. stones from the water	those who have suffered for God
8. stones from dry land	those who are righteous and faithful
9. rejected stones	sinners and those who have yet to repent
10. broken stones	those who are wicked and hypocrites

Chapters 78–110	Meaning of the Images
1. tower	church
2. built on a great, white rock	son of God
new door in the rock	new appearance of the son of God
3. built by six young men	glorious angels of God
the master of the tower	son of God
4. many helpers	other holy angels of God
5. twelve women in white	holy spirits of God as virtues
twelve women in black	vices of non-Christian living
6. ten square base stones	first generation of Christians
twenty(-five) stones	second generation of righteous people
thirty-five stones	prophets and servants of God
forty stones	prophets and teachers of the gospel
7. stones from the water	those who preached to the dead
8. stones from the mountains	different tribes of humanity
9. stones from the plain	those who are innocent in faith
10. round stones	sinners and those who are yet to repent

Chapters 78–110 (= Parable 9) contain a similar image of tower construction. Here, however, the tower is built upon an ancient rock into which a new door has been formed. The rock sits in the center of a wide plain surrounded by twelve mountains. The builders of this tower are again the six men, but they are now assisted by twelve young women in white clothing, who themselves employ the services of twelve other women in black clothing. Much of the symbolism remains the same in this picture, though the tower (= church) is now seen to be fashioned upon the rock of Christ, the doorway to salvation in the church. The women in white clothing are images of the spirit and bear the names of virtues desired by God. The women in black bear names of vices that God despises.

Obviously these two passages offer similar images of the construction of the church. The wide separation of their placement between the Visions and the Parables suggests that they may have come from separate sources. It is even possible that our author has borrowed one form of the tower image from an external source and has then constructed the other form as a literary parallel. In either case, the imagery is clear and simple as the author seeks to impress upon the reader the importance of the church for salvation.

(c) The virtues. The author of the Shepherd is quite concerned to emphasize the role of specific virtues or laudable characteristics in the life of the Christian. Lists of virtues and vices appear elsewhere in early Christian literature, of course, both in numerous passages in the New Testament and in the apostolic fathers themselves. The lists of virtues in the Shepherd appear in chapters 16, 27–45, and 92. Chapters 16 and 92 offer the virtues as names for the women who assist in the construction of the tower (= church). Chapters 27–45 form the basis for the Commandments section of the Shepherd and serve as a primary focus of the revelation offered to Hermas. It is easy to see that the author held virtues to be a vital element of early Christian faith, and that ethics and a simple lifestyle are the primary characteristics of those who have repented of their sins and now seek to be obedient to God.

(d) The Leviathan (chapters 22–24). A distinct element in the Shepherd often causes the text to be identified as an example of **apocalyptic literature.** This element appears in chapters 22–24 in the form of the *Leviathan,* the enormous beast of terror and destruction that Hermas encounters during his fourth vision. The description of this creature is meant to evoke feelings of fear and dread—fiery locusts come from the mouth of this hundred-foot beast; his head resembles a work of pottery in the colors of black, red, gold, and white. In fear Hermas prays to the Lord. In response, the charging beast is forced by the Lord's angel to stretch itself peacefully along the ground until Hermas passes along the road. As with the other visions, the church (as a woman) informs Hermas that this is an image of the coming persecution. It will be a persecution of testing. Only the pure and blameless will come through unharmed. In certain respects this imagery reflects the concept of persecution and testing portrayed in the Old Testament book of Daniel and the New Testament book of Revelation. Such imagery circulated widely during the period of the second century BC through the second century AD and was viewed as a means for understanding the events that befell Jews and Christians alike during those years.

(e) Marriage, adultery, and remarriage (chapters 29 and 32). In two related passages the author addresses specific themes associated with the relationships between married persons. Both appear within the context of Commandment 4, which is primarily concerned with the virtue of purity—especially as it is addressed by faithfulness in marriage. The author is retracing the issues of marriage, adultery, and divorce addressed by Jesus in the New Testament gospels (see Matthew 5:31–32; Mark 10:11–12; Luke 16:18). The apostle Paul also discusses a similar issue in 1 Corinthians 7:1–16, including the case of a believer's marriage to an unbeliever. The author of the Shepherd is concerned both with adultery within marriage and with the possibility of remarriage after the death of a spouse. In the case of remarriage, the author insists that it is not a sin, though greater honor and glory come to those who remain single.

With respect to the issue of marriage and adultery (chapter 29), it is readily apparent that the author is speaking to a practical issue in the Christian community. The text reveals a specific line of argument between Hermas and the shepherd. Unlike elsewhere in the writing, Hermas asks specific questions and receives specific answers. The questions are raised not simply from a concern with the case of adultery, but are offered more directly toward the issue of repentance on behalf of the offending partner. Here again we discover that the author returns to the primary theme of repentance and penance in the church. The practical implications of this theme are reflected in the passage.

(f) The sensual nature of the spirit (chapters 88, 113–14). Perhaps the most unusual and intriguing aspect of the Shepherd is the author's recurring imagery of sensuality and desire. From the outset the reader discovers that the indecisive nature of Hermas's faith is evident in his relationship to his former owner, Rhoda (see 1.1–2). After having seen her emerge from a bath in the river Tiber (near Rome), he reflects upon the happiness that such a wife could bring to him. His response might be read as less of a reflection of his lust for her than as a statement of his appreciation for her beauty and character, except that both she and an older woman (= church) then appear to him in separate visions in order to warn him against his evil designs toward Rhoda. The reader is reminded that Hermas is already married to another woman and that his goal must be to return his own family to the Lord. The primary themes of the Shepherd from this point forward revolve around the issues of a pure faith and obedience toward God, as well as around the possibility of a limited repentance for those who have broken their faithful pledges to the church.

Toward the end of the Shepherd the issues of desire and virtue resurface. During the process of the construction of the tower (= the church) in Parable 9, we read that the young women (= holy spirits) bearing the names of specific virtues and assisting in the construction entice Hermas to remain with them for a night, to sleep with them as a brother and not as a husband (chapter 88). Though Hermas desires to return to his home, the women kiss and embrace him, encourage him to play their games, and spread their outer garments upon the ground so that all may spend the night in prayer to the Lord. In this way Hermas is shown to have a pure faith—tempted more by his devotion to God than by the feminine lure of his companions. In chapters 113–14 the Shepherd informs Hermas that these women, as the holy spirits of God, will come to live in his home in order to ensure that his house will be pure and remain in God's favor.

The themes of virtue and sensual enticement are a peculiar aspect of the author's teaching. From the outset Hermas wrestles with the temptation of an inappropriate appreciation for a woman who is not his wife, while at the same time having neglected the care and nurture of his own family. Throughout the Commandments and Parables he is instructed about the importance of a pure faith and the role of virtues within a Christian lifestyle. Finally, after having been placed in a position of sensual temptation—at the enticement of the female manifestations of God's spirit!—he is promised a reward for his faith, purity, and singleminded obedience to God's will. This reward is to come in the form of the very presence of these youthful spirits of God who will soon come to live with him in his house. In a curious way, the author has moved the reader from an opening vision of potential lust—a pathway away from the will of God—to a closing promise of wholesome sensuality with God's spirit—a pathway uniting the believer with God under the guidance of the church.

8.2.9 How does the text relate to scripture?

The author of the Shepherd makes no direct appeal to scripture's authority for any of the teachings. The materials of the Shepherd—the Visions, Commandments, and Parables—are per-

sonal revelations that are given to the narrator, Hermas. This type of
presentation does not require any other specific source of authority,
such as an appeal to scripture, in order to support the authenticity of
the message itself. Instead, the mere fact that the message comes
through the divine medium of visions is sufficient authority for the
validity of the message.

At the same time, specific glimpses of biblical texts and ideas
seem to lie at the heart of various passages in the Shepherd. For
example, the *two angels* of righteousness and wickedness that control
the actions of humanity (see chapter 36) are illustrations of the
common ancient idea of the Two Ways mentality in the Old Testament books of Deuteronomy and Jeremiah, and in Barnabas 18–20
and Didache 1–6 of the apostolic fathers. So, too, the foundation
stones of the tower in Parable 9 (see 92.4) recall the patriarchs and
prophets of Old Testament history. Finally, the vision of God's
people as a vineyard of the Lord in chapter 59 is a conscious reflection of ancient Israel's understanding of itself. This picture is
painted with broad strokes in Psalm 80:8–16, Isaiah 5:1–7, and
Ezekiel 19:10–14 of the Old Testament. The New Testament continues to view early Christianity through this same imagery, as can
be seen in Matthew 20:1–16, John 15:1–11, and Romans 11:13–24.

There is little question that the Shepherd is aware of early
Christian thought reflected in New Testament literature. Some
scholars point specifically to the book of James as a possible source
for many of these ideas, while others see the use of Hebrews or
Revelation as sources. Almost certainly our author knew some or all
of the gospels of the present **canon,** even though there are virtually
no quotations from any of this material. If the Shepherd was written
in or near Rome, it is curious that there is no special dependence on
such materials, since a community like Rome undoubtedly would
have been aware of numerous early Christian writings. Likewise, if
large portions of the text were written toward the middle of the
second century, one would expect the author to have been aware of a
wide range of Christian literature. It may be best to assume that our
author, while undoubtedly aware of both Old and New Testament
literature, either was not sufficiently schooled in the use of such
texts to be able to incorporate them into the Shepherd or, perhaps,
felt no need to make any special use of this literature as a feature of
the revelations made to Hermas. In a word, while biblical themes and
ideas abound in the Shepherd, the citation of specific passages from
scripture does not.

8.3 CONTENTS

Outline of the
Materials

	Modern	Traditional	Modern	Traditional
THE VISIONS			1.1–25.7	Vis. 1–5
An introduction to Rhoda	1.1–9	Vis. 1.1.1–9		
(1) Vision of the church as an old woman	2.1–4.3	Vis. 1.2–4		
(2) Vision of the church as a younger woman	5.1–8.3	Vis. 2.1–4		
Revelation of the vision	5.1–4	Vis. 2.1		
Meaning of the book	6.1–7.4	Vis. 2.2–3		
Additional revelations	8.1–3	Vis. 2.4		
(3) Vision of the church as a youth	9.1–21.4	Vis. 3.1–13		
Revelation of the vision	9.1–10.3	Vis. 3.1.1–3.2.3		
Parable of the tower	10.4–17.10	Vis. 3.2.4–3.9.10		
Meaning of the woman's many forms	18.1–21.4	Vis. 3.10.1–3.13.4		
(4) Vision of the church as a bride	22.1–24.7	Vis. 4.1–3		
(5) Vision of the shepherd	25.1–7	Vis. 5		
THE MANDATES (OR COMMANDMENTS)			26.1–49.5	Man. 1–12
(1) On belief in God	26.1–2	Man. 1		
(2) On simplicity and innocence	27.1–7	Man. 2		
(3) On truth	28.1–5	Man. 3		
(4) On purity and relationships	29.1–32.4	Man. 4.1–4		
(5) On patience in suffering	33.1–34.8	Man. 5.1–2		
(6) On faith	35.1–36.10	Man. 6.1–2		
(7) On fear	37.1–5	Man. 7		
(8) On purity	38.1–12	Man. 8		
(9) On doubt and indecision	39.1–11	Man. 9		
(10) On grief and cheerfulness	40.1–42.4	Man. 10.1–3		
(11) On false prophets	43.1–21	Man. 11		
(12) On evil desires	44.1–45.5	Man. 12.1–2		
Final warning to keep the commandments	46.1–49.5	Man. 12.3–6		
THE SIMILITUDES (OR PARABLES)			50.1–114.5	Sim. 1–10
(1) Parable of two cities	50.1–11	Sim. 1		
(2) Parable of the vine and the elm	51.1–9	Sim. 2		
(3) Parable of trees in the winter	52.1–3	Sim. 3		
(4) Parable of trees in the summer	53.1–8	Sim. 4		
(5) Parable of the vineyard worker	54.1–60.4	Sim. 5.1–7		
(6) Parable of the two shepherds	61.1–65.7	Sim. 6.1–5		
(7) On sufferings and repentance	66.1–7	Sim. 7		
(8) Parable of the willow tree	67.1–77.5	Sim. 8.1–11		
(9) Parable of the mountains and the tower	78.1–110.3	Sim. 9.1–33		
(10) Final instructions	111.1–114.5	Sim. 10.1–4		

I, Hermas, once came to know a woman named Rhoda with whom I fell in love. In a vision she appeared to me and warned me not to have impure thoughts about her, but to pray for the guidance of God. Then she left, and I was in terror. While in this state I had a vision of a second woman. She offered this same warning and further insisted that I should convert my entire family to God's will. She then read to me from the Psalms—and my vision ended.

A year later I had a second vision at the same place. Again the woman appeared, and she gave me words of wisdom from a book to share with God's followers. With time the meaning of the book was revealed to me. And the message was again that my family must return to God, that all of those who have sinned will be forgiven, because salvation comes to those who are innocent and live a simple lifestyle. I came to understand that this woman was the church—the first of God's creation. And once again in a vision, she came to give me further instructions about the wisdom of the book.

In yet a third vision the woman returned, and I sat on her left side. She explained that the seat on her right was saved for those who had suffered for God. She showed me a tower being built by many men. This tower represented the church, she explained, and then she answered all of my many questions about the manner of its construction. Around the tower stood seven women whose qualities were faith, purity, simplicity, knowledge, innocence, reverence, and love. The woman charged me to warn the people of the church that they must avoid greed and should work for the good of the poor. So, too, the leaders must be at peace among themselves and act as worthy servants of the Lord. And as I came to accept this message, I understood why it was that with each vision this woman—the church—had become a more youthful and energetic figure.

Some twenty days later I saw a vision of a huge animal in my path—the Leviathan. But with prayer and trust I passed by unharmed. Soon I met the church once more, though this time she appeared as a radiant bride. She explained the meaning of the beast, and observed that I had escaped its fury because of my faith in God. She charged me to warn other believers to prepare themselves to trust God during the coming days of testing.

In a final vision a man dressed as a shepherd—the angel of repentance—appeared and told me to live by the following twelve commandments and to record them in a book: Believe that there is

Summary of the Argument

only one God. Have simplicity and live as an innocent child. Love truth, and let your thoughts be good and true. Be pure in your heart and faithful in your relationships. (Here he explained the way in which spouses should relate to one another, as well as the possibility of forgiveness for those who have sinned—even after their baptism.) Have courage and suffer trials with patience through God's spirit. Have faith in that good angel who wrestles the evil spirit within you. Fear the Lord and revere his commandments. Avoid all evils while choosing to do the good. Do not be uncertain in your decisions or hesitate to ask God for anything. Do not let grief destroy the spirit of God within you, but be filled with joy. Resist false prophets, whose evil ways reveal the empty course of their teachings. Avoid the many forms of evil desire. So it was that the shepherd warned me to be careful to keep all of these commandments.

To illustrate the need for care in such matters, I was offered further guidance through the imagery of several parables. Thus I learned that our real home is in another city and that we should not place great value in the city and lands where we now live. Likewise, just as the vine depends upon the elm tree to be a place where it may bear its fruit, the rich person should share with the poor so that both may receive their salvation from God. As trees look all the same in the winter, yet reveal their fruits in the summer, in this world it is difficult to distinguish the sinner from the righteous person—but in the coming world all will be clear. The shepherd warned me not to fast in vain but, like the servant who faithfully tended his master's vineyard and distributed his reward among his friends, to fast in a way acceptable to God and to remain pure.

Later the shepherd returned to me in a vision and offered yet more parables for my understanding. He showed me two shepherds, the first of which made his sheep fat and carefree and the second of which snatched those sheep and entangled them in thorns—so too will those who now live in luxury and deceit receive punishment at the hands of the Lord. When I asked him to remove the shepherd of punishment from my own house, he observed that suffering in this life was a sign of what was to come and that my faith in the commandments of the Lord would bring these trials to an end. Then he showed me an angel who took the branches from a willow tree and gave them to all peoples. In their hands some branches flourished, while others withered. The tree was God's law—that is, God's Son preached to all people. Those in whom this law grew were gathered into a tower, while the rest planted their branches. Again, those for whom the branches grew were also gathered into the tower. Thus it is that those who are righteous are gathered together by God, whether they are pure or have repented of their sins.

Finally, the shepherd took me to Arcadia where I could see a plain surrounded by twelve different mountains. In the middle of the plain was an ancient rock with a new door. The door was encircled by twelve young women. Six men then approached and directed the construction of a huge stone tower upon the rock. When it was finished, the Lord of the tower came and tested the structure as to its worth. Any rejected stones were given to the shepherd to be cleaned and reshaped in order to be included once more into the tower walls. Those unusable stones were then returned to the mountains by women in black clothing. Throughout this process I helped the shepherd and enjoyed the company of those young women who assisted him. I came to understand that the new door was the Son of God—the rock—through whom all people may enter God's kingdom. Upon that rock was built the tower of the church, as was directed by the Son of God with the angels and holy spirits. The meaning of the stones was revealed and that of the mountains which was their source. For each represented the many workers in God's kingdom. Yet some stones were defective, and these represented those who have fallen away from God's teachings. Each mountain produced different stones—some of value, others of little worth. But the stones that were taken from the plain were among the best. The shepherd instructed me to remain pure, to let my own life be shaped into a stone of value.

When all was revealed, the angel who had entrusted me to the shepherd instructed me to live according to the shepherd's direction. I was shown to be a faithful servant and was given the ten young women—God's holy spirits—to keep my house pure in all respects. I was charged to witness to other people on behalf of the Lord's teachings.

8.4 RELATED LITERATURE

Barnard, L. W. "Hermas, the Church and Judaism." In *Studies in the Apostolic Fathers and their Background.* Pages 161–63. New York: Schocken, 1966. (BQ1080.B366 1966)

———. "The Shepherd of Hermas in Recent Study." *Heythrop Journal* 9 (1, 1968), pp. 29–36.

Jeffers, James S. *Conflict at Rome: Social Order and Hierarchy in Early Christianity.* Minneapolis: Fortress, 1991. (BR878.R7.J44 1991)

Lake, Kirsopp. "The Shepherd of Hermas and Christian Life in Rome in the Second Century." *Harvard Theological Review* 4 (1, 1911), pp. 25–46.

Osiek, Carolyn. *Rich and Poor in the* Shepherd of Hermas: *An Exegetical-Social Investigation.* Catholic Biblical Quarterly Monograph Series 15. Washington, D.C.: Catholic Biblical Association, 1983. (BS2900.H5.O74 1983)

Pernveden, Lage. *The Concept of the Church in the Shepherd of Hermas.* Translated by Ingrid Reeves and Nigel Reeves. Studia Theological Lundensia 27. Lund: G.W.K. Gleerup, 1966. (BS2900.H5.P4 1966)

Reiling, J. *Hermas and Christian Prophecy: A Study of the Eleventh Mandate.* Supplements to Novum Testamentum 37. Leiden: E. J. Brill, 1973. (BQ1506.P7.R4 1973)

Seitz, Oscar J. F. "Relationship of the Shepherd to the Epistle of James." *Journal of Biblical Literature* 63 (2, 1944), pp. 131-40.

Snyder, Graydon F. *The Shepherd of Hermas.* The Apostolic Fathers 6. New York: Thomas Nelson & Sons, 1968. (BQ1080.A4 1964)

Wilson, J. Christian. *Toward a Reassessment of the Shepherd of Hermas: Its Date and Its Pneumatology.* Lewiston, N.Y.: Edwin Mellen, 1993. (BS2900.H5.W55 1993)

9 The Letter to Diognetus

9.1.1   Manuscript tradition—one known Greek text (destroyed by fire)

9.1.2   Literary form—early Christian letter constructed from two separate documents

9.1.3   Authorship—unknown non-Jewish Christian

9.1.4   Date—AD 117–310 (probably middle to late second century)

9.1.5   Setting—unknown

9.1.6   Purpose—to defend the Christian faith (chapters 1–10); for use as a homily for a specific event of Christian worship (chapters 11–12)

9.1.7   Primary elements—invalid nature of non-Christian worship; church—knowledge—mysticism

9.1.8   Special images—Christians as the soul of the world; observing the heavens; garden of paradise

9.1.9   Relationship to scripture—no focus upon the Old Testament; some dependence upon the themes of Paul and the theology of the Gospel of John

9.2.1 Where did we get our text?

Unlike the majority of writings from the apostolic fathers, the Letter to Diognetus is known only from a single copy in Greek. This text was preserved together with a copy of four other writings from the early church theologian **Justin Martyr** in the Codex Argentoratensis Graec. ix, a manuscript of the thirteenth or fourteenth century. Although privately owned during the early sixteenth century, the **codex** soon became the property of the Alsatian monastery of Maursmünster. Eventually the text was housed in Strassburg, Germany, where it unfortunately was lost to fire in 1870 during the Franco-German War.

Prior to the destruction of the text, scholars made at least five copies. From these copies it is obvious that the original manuscript contained many problems with respect to wording. Portions of our present translation have been reconstructed from the Strassburg manuscript while various sections of the letter are modern attempts to complete gaps in the text.

9.2.2 What form does the text take?

Most scholars believe that the text is the compilation of two different documents which originally circulated separately. The first of the documents is a letter that is preserved in chapters 1–10. The second, in chapters 11–12, is a fragment of an early Christian homily or treatise. Scholars have two reasons to think that the Letter to Diognetus was originally two separate sources:

(a) There is a brief gap at the conclusion of chapter 10. If chapters 1–10 once formed an actual letter, as the structure and focus of the text seem to suggest, this gap may indicate that the original conclusion to that letter was lost or discarded when chapters 11–12 were added. There is no reason to think that other sections of the letter were lost as well, however, since the author's argument reaches a logical conclusion by the end of chapter 10.

(b) There is a marked shift in literary style and theological focus between chapters 1–10 and chapters 11–12. Clearly chapters 1–10 follow the typical approach of an early Christian **apology,** a form of literature designed to defend Christians and their faith against potential opponents. The materials of chapters 11–12, on the other hand, appear to preserve a portion of an ancient theological treatise, probably derived from an early Christian homily.

With regard to the history of transmission, there is no discernable reason why the two sources were combined. In other, similar instances, texts have become linked when the source of the writings was forgotten. This occasionally occurred when documents were copied onto a single papyrus or parchment roll, or **codex,** perhaps as a way to save space. Whatever the reason for its present form, the Letter to Diognetus itself suggests that our author (or editor) found the two sources similar enough to be combined into a single work.

9.2.3 Who was the author?

The letter in its current form does not name its author. The argument against Judaism in 3.1–4.6, however, suggests that the author was not Jewish. By the same token, no author is listed for either of the two apparent sources lying behind the present text. If chapters 1–10 originally formed an early Christian letter whose conclusion has since been lost, then it is quite likely that the author's name was appended to the concluding materials and subsequently was lost with them. There is no reason to think that any name was ever attached to the homily fragment in chapters 11–12.

Since the letter itself is no help in identifying a specific author, scholars usually approach the problem on the basis of external information. On the one hand, the Codex Argentoratensis Graec. ix, which assumes that the entire text was the work of a single individual, indicates that the letter was from **Justin Martyr.** Thus the letter was included with other of his writings. The style of the **apology** in chapters 1–10 does indeed resemble similar works associated with **Justin.** On the other hand, a similar style occurs in the writings of the second-century apologists **Aristides** and **Tatian,** the latter of whom was a student of **Justin.**

If, as scholars suggest, chapters 11–12 should be attributed to a separate author, then numerous other writers from the period of the first through ninth centuries may have produced these materials. Several names from the second century arise in typical discussions of the issue. For example, there are intriguing parallels between these chapters and the fragmentary homily which survives from the writings of **Melito of Sardis.** Some scholars argue, however, that these chapters represent the conclusion of the lost text of the *Philosophumena* by **Hippolytus,** who lived and worked in Rome. Perhaps the most interesting suggestion is that the letter is the famous *Apology of Quadratus* that was addressed to the emperor **Hadrian** early in the second century. This text has been lost, except for a short fragment preserved by **Eusebius of Caesarea** in *Ecclesiastical History* 4.3.1–2. Finally, arguments are also made on behalf of the names of **Theophilus,** a bishop of Antioch, and **Pantaenus,** the founder of the famous catechetical school of ancient Alexandria.

Ultimately, it is impossible to identify with confidence any specific author or authors behind the text. The frequent distinction made between the author of chapters 1–10 and that of chapters 11–12 may even be irrelevant, since it is quite possible that the same person wrote the two texts on different occasions. Furthermore, the question of authorship assumes from the outset that the letter circulated in the public forum. It is certainly possible, however, that the text was simply a theological exercise produced by an early Christian student—a *homework assignment!* Perhaps one can say only that the letter reveals the work of a cultured mind-set and bears the signs of a classical education combined with a developed literary style. The identity of the early Christian who produced this work will probably remain a mystery.

9.2.4 When was the text written?	The date of our letter, as well as of its sources, is unknown. The range of possibilities spans the period 117–310. Typically the date of composition is determined by postulating a particular author, which is most difficult in this case. Four factors lead us to assume that the text was composed in the latter half of the second century: (a) There is no reference to the Holy Spirit throughout the discussion, a typical omission among second-century authors. (b) The lack of concern for the personal nature of the Word of God in Christian living was a primary concern among the authors of the third century. (c) The text's concerted effort to devalue Judaism suggests that the author was aware of the struggles between Judaism and Christianity during the middle of the second century. (d) Finally, the perspective of the author was somewhat universal in nature, which suggests that time had elapsed since the initial rise of Christianity throughout the Roman Empire. While none of these elements is conclusive in its own right, the combination of factors suggests a composition within the late second-century church.
9.2.5 In what setting was the text written?	It is impossible to determine a single setting for the text. For example, the letter of chapters 1–10 may have originated in a city different from the homily of chapters 11–12. Furthermore, the place where these two sources were combined may have been in yet another site. Most scholars situate the text to correspond with the location of their proposed author. In this matter there is no uniform agreement.
9.2.6 Why was the text written?	Because the text appears to be written for use on two separate occasions, it is perhaps best to discuss the purpose of the writing in accordance with each section individually: (a) The letter (chapters 1–10). This text, which eventually defined the final form of the writing, is presented as an **apology** or letter in defense of Christianity. It is directed to the unknown

recipient Diognetus, who appears either to have held some official post within a local government or to have been a representative of the Roman Empire. Some scholars suggest that Diognetus was the teacher of the second-century emperor **Marcus Aurelius** to whom the author appeals. Other scholars contend that the name Diognetus refers to the procurator Claudius Diogenes of Alexandria (197–203); this undergirds the position that **Pantaenus** authored the work. In neither case is there any conclusive data to support these conjectures. While the letter may originally have been addressed to a single individual, the text's general nature suggests that its author intended that it would eventually circulate among a wider audience.

(b) The homily (chapters 11–12). Chapters 11–12 appear to form a portion of an ancient Christian homily composed either for the season of Epiphany or for Easter. Some scholars assert that the phrase "He is the eternal one, who today is accounted a son" (11.5) indicates that the homily was delivered at the Feast of the Nativity. This seems to be unlikely, however, since this feast generally was not distinguished from other Christian festivals in antiquity. There is no evidence that any specific audience is intended here.

The division of the letter into two separate sources assists in defining the primary themes of the author. The brief nature of these two sections also helps to delimit the discussion:

9.2.7 What are the primary traits of the text?

(a) The invalid nature of non-Christian worship. The essence of chapters 1–10 is contained in the author's argument to Diognetus that non-Christian patterns of worship, whether pagan or Jewish, are inadequate. Thus in chapter 2 the dumb idols of pagan religion are shown to be fraudulent. They cannot protect themselves, much less intervene in the affairs of humans. On the other hand, the pious falsehoods of Judaism are exposed in chapters 3–4, where it is claimed that the Jews also have turned the one, true God into an image of idolatry. For the author, the Christian message of God supersedes all other forms of religious devotion. Salvation comes through God's Christ alone. Humanity can aspire to worship God in true purity and faith through Christ alone.

(b) Church, knowledge, mysticism (chapters 11–12). A distinct triad of themes dominates the homily of the final chapters. The author insists that God sent the Word—God's Son—in order to enrich *the church*. Through this very institution "the faith of the gospels is established, the tradition of the apostles is guarded, and the grace of the church glories" (11.6). A vital aspect of participation in the church comes through the recognition of *knowledge*. The knowledge of God's teaching is a gift for those who would believe—yet it is not to be used except in the purity of faith. Finally, both church and knowledge are depicted in the light of a *mysticism* that interprets the work of God in the world in a way that defies the common concerns of daily living. The author admits that the words of salvation that come through the church and through knowledge may seem strange to the listener (11.1). Yet the true believer can come to understand them with the assistance of God. Chapters 11–12 thus strongly emphasize the theological concepts of church, knowledge, and mysticism. Such themes already were available to early Christians from the Gospel of John. This gospel may even have shaped our author's own focus.

9.2.8 What special images appear?

While the text of the Letter to Diognetus is not extensive, it contains several interesting images:

(a) Christians as the soul of the world (chapter 6). The author poses an intriguing analogy with respect to the role and function of Christians within the world by comparing the role of the church in the world to the place of the soul in the body. Although it is not of the body, the soul inhabits the body and directs its actions; yet the body resists this direction because the desires of the flesh are frustrated by the soul's will. In certain respects the body is a prison for the soul. With time, however, the mortal body must fail and the immortal soul can be released. In each description of the soul the author envisions the lives and activities of Christians who seek to serve the will of God within the world. The influence of Christianity is great, and those who persecute the faithful followers of God in fact only serve to strengthen the faithful's resolve to share the Christian message of salvation.

(b) Observing the heavens (4.5; 7.2). The question of the movement of heavenly bodies is raised twice. As part of the rebuke of Judaism in chapters 3–4, the author condemns the Jews for their zealous "attention to the stars and moon" (4.5) which mark the seasons and establish religious festivals. Diognetus is informed that such observances are arbitrary and hold no value as proofs of piety. Indeed, the author believes that any attempt to interpret the will of

God, who is the creator of the heavens, by the creation itself must necessarily be flawed. So too, the faith of the Jews is flawed.

The second reference to the heavens appears at 7.2, when the author confesses that God is indeed the creator of the world. God directs both the sun and the moon to shine at the appropriate times and sets the stars "to follow the course of the moon." This last observation is curious, of course, since the stars do not actually follow the moon across the sky. Yet, presumably, our author assumes that the moon, as the guiding light of the night sky, holds authority over the light of the stars.

These references to the heavens and to the role of God in both the creation and the direction of heavenly bodies suggest that the author was concerned for the claims of astrology. The author rejects any attempt to interpret the seasons by the movement of the heavens. At the same time, the author recognizes that God is the creator of all things and gives authority to the lights of the sky. Such statements suggest that the author wanted Christianity to be viewed both as a reflection of worldly wisdom and as a religion of devout faith.

(c) Garden of paradise (chapter 12). In the letter's concluding homily (chapters 11–12), the reader discovers the image of the garden of paradise from Genesis 3 in the Old Testament. The garden illustrates the potential hope and strength that the love of God can bestow upon the true believer. Unlike the trees in the Genesis account, the fruit of the "tree of knowledge" and the "tree of life" are no longer forbidden. They are available for all to take and enjoy. Yet their true value may only be recognized in the work of the pure in heart. As the author notes, the serpent of disobedience forever threatens those who would take what is not rightfully theirs from the garden.

The Letter of Diognetus refers to scripture only a few times, with virtually no reference to the Old Testament. At first glance this seems striking for a text traditionally dated to the latter half of the second century. Yet there may be a reasonable explanation for this omission.

With respect to the absence of Old Testament citations, it is only natural that the author of chapters 1–10 would refrain from depending on the scriptures of Judaism, since the teachings of the Jewish tradition were rejected in chapters 3–4. It is true that the characterization of God as the one "who made heaven and earth and

9.2.9 How does the text relate to scripture?

all that is in them" (3.4) echoes Exodus 20:11 or perhaps Psalm 146:6. Yet these words were a common, stock description of God in early Christianity. The same phrase appears, for example, in Acts 14:15, which may also have been in the mind of our author. In a similar way, the descriptions of the Lord's appearance as the messiah of Israel from Zechariah 9:9 and Malachi 3:2 (see Diognetus 7.3–6) represent typical characterizations of Jesus of Nazareth in early Christian circles. One should assume that the author uses these descriptions without any concern for their Old Testament origins.

As mentioned above, Diognetus 12 describes the garden of paradise from Genesis 3. This image forms part of the homily, however, and should not necessarily be associated with the original letter to Diognetus (chapters 1–10). Even if some connection with the letter could be made, the original intention of the author of Genesis—to indicate that humanity rebelled against God by eating forbidden fruit—is being reinterpreted. Such fruit is now available to all who hear the good news of Christ and are willing to use the knowledge and life it brings in the spirit of obedient faith.

With respect to the New Testament, there are no specific citations in chapters 1–10, unless Acts 14:15 lies behind the quotation in 3.2. It is quite possible that the author simply assumed widely recognized themes from the letters of Paul and the gospels, though these are never clearly stated. At the same time, there is no question that the letter's structure is different from that of the Pauline model—a form adopted by most early Christian letters, including the letters of Ignatius and Polycarp. With reference to New Testament themes and literary style, therefore, we possess no evidence that the author was drawing from any particular text.

The homily of chapters 11–12 reflects an obvious concern for Pauline thought and for the theology of the Gospel of John. In 12.5 the author quotes from 1 Corinthians 8:1 ("Knowledge puffs up, but love builds up") and attributes it specifically to "the apostle" (Paul). In addition, these two chapters show a marked dependence on the theology of the Gospel of John and the letter of 1 John. This theology characteristically focuses on Christ as the Word of God, emphasizes the value of Christian knowledge, and highlights the role of divine revelation in the developing church. This trend toward a broader dependence upon Johannine theology began to surface in Christian communities toward the end of the second century. It clearly is a popular perspective with the author of our homily fragment.

9 . 3   C O N T E N T S

*Outline of the
Materials*

*Summary of the
Argument*

I write to you Diognetus in order to answer your questions about this new religion of Christianity. Open your mind to the situation, if you will.

Let us consider the gods of the pagans. Are these figures not the work of people like us? Indeed, these idols are made of stone, metal, wood, and clay—substances that can easily be reshaped into another form. How foolish it is to worship and to offer sacrifices to these figures which cannot avoid rust or rot, which must be locked away at night in order not to be stolen. Is it any wonder that Christians refuse to honor and worship such so-called gods?

Yet, neither do Christians worship in the same way as the Jews. Even the Jews have come to treat the one, true God as though this too were some deity who needed care. Jewish sacrifices and offerings closely resemble the work of the pagans. The Jewish concerns over food, circumcision, fasts, and feasts—which are randomly determined by the movement of the stars—come from foolishness and pride. Would you expect Christians to follow such shallow human teachings?

No, Christians are different. They appear everywhere in the world, yet are truly citizens of the land of heaven. They live as other people do, but work for the benefit of all nations. Nevertheless, they are persecuted by Jews and Greeks alike—though no good reason is ever given. As the soul lives in the body, so Christians live in the world. The body contends with the soul; the world rejects Christians. Yet the soul loves the body and is confined within it. Similarly, Christians, who live within this mortal realm, work to improve the world. And why is this? Because they see that God has revealed a message through the words of a unique messenger—Christ. Christ was not sent as a judge but as one who came to call others to God. Those who respond to this call get stronger in the face of adversity.

Before Christ came, people accepted foolish philosophies of life and misunderstood who God really was. Yet God revealed all things to Christ, who then shared them with us. And though we were slow to hear his words and we resisted in our ignorance, he was patient and forgiving. Christ even offered himself in our place as a human sacrifice by which our sins could be pardoned by God. So it is only natural that we honor him and find our strength in him.

You too, Diognetus, can share in this knowledge of forgiveness. If you choose to imitate God, you will find that happiness does not come through power or wealth, but in the ways that you might choose to help other people. And you too will become a citizen of heaven.

I speak here only as a witness to what I have found to be true about God and about Christ whom God sent to all of us. God is eternal and has been revealed throughout history—first through fear, then through grace, and finally through faith. Now I share God's plain message of love with you. God has truly planted a garden with many fruits for those who love truth—a garden which bears both the tree of knowledge and the tree of life. Understand this, that both are good to eat! They become unacceptable only when people choose to be disobedient to God's call for a life of purity. So it is that God's gifts of knowledge and life must be tempered by obedience in order to be correctly understood. These fruits are available to all believers and their appropriate use in light of God's message of salvation brings glory to the Father. Amen.

9.4   RELATED   LITERATURE

Andriessen, P. "The Authorship of the Epistula ad Diognetum." *Vigiliae Christianae* 1 (2, 1947), pp. 129–36.

Barnard, L. W. "The Epistle ad Diognetum: Two Units from One Author?" *Zeitschrift für die neutestamentliche Wissenschaft* 56 (2, 1965), pp. 130–37.

Connolly, R. H. "The Date and Authorship of the Epistle to Diognetus." *Journal of Theological Studies* 36 (4, 1935), pp. 347–53.

_____. "Ad Diognetum xi–xii." *Journal of Theological Studies* 37 (1, 1936), pp. 2–15.

Grant, Robert M. *Greek Apologists of the Second Century.* Pages 178–89. Philadelphia: Westminster Press, 1988. (BT1115.G7 1988)

Lienhard, Joseph T. "The Christology of the Epistle to Diognetus." *Vigiliae Christianae* 24 (4, 1970), pp. 280–89.

Meecham, H. G. *The Epistle to Diognetus.* Manchester: Manchester University Press, 1949. (BQ1273.M4 1949)

O'Neill, J. G. "The Epistle to Diognetus." *Irish Ecclesiastical Record* 85 (1, 1956), pp. 92–106.

Thierry, J. J. "The Logos as Teacher in ad Diognetum XI, 1." *Vigiliae Christianae* 20 (2, 1966), pp. 146–49.

Townsley, A. L. "Notes for an Interpretation of the Epistle to Diognetus." *Rivista di studi classici* 24 (1, 1976), pp. 5–20.

Glossary

allegorical method—An approach to scripture that searches for the presence of allegories (symbols or representations of truths) within the text. Though broadly applied in the early church, the method is most widely associated with the catechetical school of Alexandria during the third and fourth centuries AD. The attempt to find hidden scriptural truths appears to have entered Christianity through its contact with Jewish scholars influenced by Greek philosophy.

Anicetus (died ca. AD 166)—Bishop of Rome from ca. 155 until his death some eleven years later. The life and leadership of Anicetus are unclear, though he is known to have met with the bishop Polycarp and to have lived in Rome while Justin Martyr, Hegesippus, and the gnostic Valentinus were active in the city. It is likely that he was responsible for the construction of the original shrine for the apostle Peter on the Vatican hill.

apocalyptic literature—A form of writing which employs images of the end time as its primary concern, often in creative and lively images. Typical characteristics of this literature include a belief in two oppositional cosmic powers, a division of time into two distinct ages (the present age of evil and the future age of promise), and a vision or "revelation" (*apocalypse* means disclosure) about future events. Such literature was common among ancient religions, including Judaism, and broadly influenced later Christian thought and theology.

Apocrypha—A collection of texts from the biblical period that did not gain the universal status of scripture within the Jewish-Christian tradition. There are two basic collections of Apocrypha: the Old Testament Apocrypha were generally written prior to the destruction of Jerusalem in AD 70; the New Testament Apocrypha were composed during the second to ninth centuries. Both sets of materials attest to the continued development of early Jewish and early Christian traditions.

apology—Beginning in the second century AD, early Christianity produced writings designed to offer a reasoned defense of Christian faith and actions. These *apologies* often were directed toward specific circumstances and to named individuals. Sometimes they were written as general defenses of the early Christian movement, occasionally as an answer to philosophical challenges or the claims of competing religions.

Apostolic Constitutions—A late, fourth-century compilation of early Christian materials reflecting texts and traditions from the churches of ancient Syria. Included here are portions of the *Didascalia Apostolorum*, the Didache, and the *Apostolic Tradition* by the bishop Hippolytus. Most of the text is concerned with issues of church structure and order, though subthemes from early Christianity abound.

Aristides (early second-century AD)—Aristides was a Christian theologian from the city of Athens, Greece. We know from Eusebius of Caesarea that his *Apology* was directed toward the emperor Hadrian around the year 125, though another version of the work addresses it to Antoninus Pius (138–61). Aristides defended Christianity against the beliefs of the pagans, as well as against the rejection of Christ by the Jews.

Athanasius of Alexandria (ca. AD 300–373)—Elected as bishop of Alexandria in 328, Athanasius authored numerous letters and theological reflections. His career was complicated by his support of the Council of Nicaea (325) against the teachings of the priest Arius. He is most famous for his involvement in political struggles with the emperor of Constantinople (modern Istanbul), which resulted in nearly sixteen years in exile.

atonement—By general definition, atonement indicates a reconciliation between two parties. In the Jewish-Christian tradition it refers to the restoration of the broken relationship between God and humanity. The early Christian images of atonement were derived from the Old Testament's portrayal of divine forgiveness as coming through the ritual sacrifices of the priests of God.

Augustine of Hippo (AD 354–430)—Unquestionably the foremost theologian and author among early bishops, Augustine was trained in rhetoric and followed the teachings of Mani before he converted to Christianity in his thirties. As the bishop of the North African city of Hippo, he wrote extensively about his own Christian experiences, in defiance of heretical threats toward an orthodox faith, and about questions of theology and faith. His influence on later thought has few parallels in church history.

canon—A term denoting a standard or primary collection of texts with special authority for a specific religious tradition. The Hebrew Scriptures developed as a canon of authority for the faith of Judaism. Early Christianity, which recognized these same Jewish writings as authoritative and came to know them as the Old Testament, collected additional writings from early Christian authors into a second canon commonly called the New Testament.

Clement of Alexandria (ca. AD 160–215)—Though born in Athens, Greece, Clement became an important author and theologian in early Christian Egypt. He perhaps is best known for his leadership of the famous catechetical school of Alexandria, which was associated with the renowned library of that city. His extensive writings endorse the typically Egyptian *logos* Christology and the allegorical interpretation of scripture.

codex—The earliest variation of what scholars now classify as a book form. Ancient versions of the codex gained popularity in Egypt, particularly among Christians, as a useful replacement for the traditional papyrus scroll. The codex was fashioned from unrolled scrolls that had been cut into short lengths, folded, and stitched at a center fold in order to form pages. Pieces of leather reinforced with scrap papyrus often functioned as a cover or binder for the pages.

Codex Alexandrinus (Codex A, fifth century AD)—One of the most noteworthy biblical manuscripts of antiquity, this text preserves our chief copy of 1–2 Clement. After its discovery in Alexandria in the year 1098, the codex was taken to Constantinople (modern Istanbul) in the seventeenth century. Eventually (1757) the British Library of London acquired it.

Codex Hierosolymitanus (Codex H, eleventh century AD)—A late Greek manuscript preserving portions of scripture and several writings from the apostolic fathers. This work is best known as

the only source for the entire text of the Didache. This manuscript was originally known as Codex Constantinopolitanus and
referred to as C.

Codex Sinaiticus (Codex ℵ, fourth century AD)—A significant
Greek manuscript from the early church and one of the two
primary witnesses for the so-called Alexandrian text of biblical
transmission. Prepared by skilled editors in the scholarly tradition of Alexandria, Egypt, this codex represents one of the best
forms of the original New Testament writings. The work was
discovered at St. Catherine's Monastery on Mount Sinai in
1844.

Constantine the Great (ca. AD 285–337)—Emperor of Rome during the years 306–337, Constantine assisted the church in its
quest for legal status within the Roman Empire. He was greatly
influenced by his mother, Helena, who herself was a Christian.
An able soldier and ruler, Constantine undertook an active role
in the development of the institutional church and ruled during
many of its theological controversies.

creeds—Confessions of faith officially sanctioned by a religious
organization. In early Christian literature these were usually
short, though their length increased in correlation with the
history of the church. The purpose of a creed is to define a
common faith and theology for those who worship together, as
well as to identify those not in full agreement with that core
belief.

Cyprian (ca. AD 200–258)—A bishop of Carthage during the middle of the third century, Cyprian came from a distinguished
local family. He is best known for his numerous letters depicting
the life of the church during the persecutions under the late
Roman Empire. As a result of his continued conflict with the
church at Rome, Cyprian eventually was exiled to Curubis
before his trial and execution under the proconsul Galerius
Maximus.

decalogue—Also known as the Ten Commandments, this passage of
scripture represents a summary of the covenant agreement between the God of Israel and the Hebrew people on Mount Sinai.
The wording of the text appears in two places in the Old
Testament—Exodus 20 and Deuteronomy 5.

Didymus the Blind (AD 313–398)—Though little is known about his early life, this blind scholar became the leader of the famous catechetical school of religious instruction at Alexandria during the reign of the bishop Athanasius. A biblical authority and prominent theologian, Didymus appears to have written extensively. Unfortunately, only a few of his works remain today.

docetism—Based upon a Greek word meaning "to seem," this prominent third-century heresy taught that the humanity of Jesus of Nazareth was only apparent and not real. The early church debated this issue vigorously, since such claims denied that Jesus had truly suffered and died as a human being. Docetism, a primary feature of early gnostic theologies, persists today in the popular mind-set of Christianity.

Domitian (AD 51–96)—Emperor of Rome during the years 81–96, Domitian is recognized by historians for his ruthless opposition to suspected opponents. He authorized the universal persecution of Christians, and numerous early Christian texts depict the terror of his reign. Some scholars speculate that the husband of his niece Domitilla wrote the letter we know as 1 Clement.

dualism—The view that reality may be divided into two essential forces. There are two forms of this understanding. From a cosmic perspective, the world struggles between two opposing forces—typically, one of evil and one of good. From a philosophical approach, the essence of a person is divided between two incompatible natures—that of the body and that of the soul. Early Christianity incorporated both views from those religions and philosophies into which it came in contact.

Epiphanius (ca. AD 315–403)—Bishop of Salamis in Cyprus at the end of the fourth century, Epiphanius is best remembered for his attempts to refute the heresies of the period. His work, known as the *Panarion*, provides valuable information about the theological struggles in early Christian circles. He opposed the teachings of Origen of Alexandria and supported the views of the Council of Nicaea.

episcopacy—A term derived from the Greek word for "overseer" or "bishop." The episcopacy indicates the historical succession of bishops or the authority of a bishop in any particular city or geographical location. The roots of the episcopacy in early Christianity are not clear, though it is unlikely that the oversight of particular church communities by a single individual developed in a uniform manner.

eschatology—The doctrine of the last things. In a narrow sense the term implies an understanding of the end of history and time which permits for the salvation of some and for the destruction of others. In a broad sense the idea suggests the transition of reality from an older state to an entirely new and different existence, yet within the framework of history. Most early Christian literature was composed with some eschatological understanding of history.

eucharist—A central sacrament of the Christian liturgy featuring the consumption of bread and wine in memory of the death and resurrection of Jesus of Nazareth. The word comes from the word *eucharistia*, the Greek term for "thanksgiving," and eventually came to identify a specific liturgical occasion within the early church in distinction to the *agape* or "love feast" tradition.

Eusebius of Caesarea (ca. AD 260–ca. 340)—Bishop of Caesarea from 313 until his death, Eusebius was author of the most important historical record of the early church, the well-known *Ecclesiastical History*. His writings reflect the theological debates and controversies of the early fourth century and preserve portions of numerous ancient documents, many of which have since been lost.

gnosticism—An early religious movement which believed that a specific "knowledge" or *gnosis* could be obtained as a key to human salvation. With its roots in both Jewish theology and Greek philosophy, this movement gained a wide following among early Christians and became popular within Egyptian Christianity. Eventually, specific schools of gnosticism and their teachers were rejected by the mainstream church as inconsistent with an orthodox Christian faith.

Gospel of the Egyptians—Preserved only as scattered fragments in the writings of Clement of Alexandria, this early Christian gospel circulated among churches during the second century. Little is known about the text itself, and nothing about its author. Another manuscript by the same title appears in a collection of writings from Nag Hammadi, Egypt, though the two texts appear to be different compositions.

Gospel of Thomas—An early gospel text of the late-first to mid-second century. This writing features sayings of the resurrected Jesus which purportedly were revealed in secret to the author. Unlike the New Testament gospels, this text contains no passion narrative and lacks any emphasis on the life and works of Jesus of Nazareth. The only complete copy is preserved in Coptic together with a collection of other texts from Nag Hammadi, Egypt.

Gregory of Nyssa (AD 331–ca. 395)—A bishop in the region of Cappadocia (western Turkey) who, together with Basil of Caesarea and Gregory of Nazianzus, became known as one of the "three great Cappadocians." A major defender against Arianism as advocated by Eunomius of Cyzicus, Gregory of Nyssa wrote extensively on numerous issues of speculative theology. His influence upon subsequent Christian theologians continued well into the twelfth century.

Hadrian (AD 76–118)—Emperor of Rome during the years 117–138, Hadrian was concerned to fortify the borders of the empire against the threat of hostile tribes. Examples of his building efforts in this endeavor may be found throughout Europe and the Middle East even today. Though generally tolerant of religious views, Hadrian allowed the martyrdom of Christians during his reign.

Hippolytus of Rome (ca. AD 170–ca. 236)—A leading theologian, Hippolytus became the bishop of a Christian community in Rome which had separated from the main church. He was a prominent author whose most famous works include the *Refutation of All Heresies* and the *Apostolic Tradition*. Hippolytus, though not an imaginative thinker, sought to defend the pure faith against those persons in the church who had sinned after baptism.

incipit—Introductory words appearing at the beginning of ancient and Medieval manuscripts. By tradition, the first words of a work typically were used as the title. Works which were written upon a piece of papyrus often were rolled for storage or transport, at which time these words were written on the outside for the purpose of identification. The practice served in effect to move the words to the end of the work.

Irenaeus (ca. AD 115–ca. 202)—Born in Smyrna of Asia Minor, Irenaeus eventually became an early bishop in the city of Lyons. He is widely known as an associate of the bishop Polycarp. Irenaeus's extensive writings addressed the rising threat of gnosticism, as well as the need to observe the appropriate apostolic traditions. He vigorously defended the early Christian scriptures and championed the authority of the church in the life of every Christian.

Jerome (ca. AD 347–420)—A premier scripture scholar and translator, Jerome is best known for his Latin translation of the scriptures—the Vulgate. He traveled extensively around the Mediterranean world and authored numerous responses to the writings of those he visited. His commentaries on scripture were well known and respected among Medieval scholars.

John Chrysostom (ca. AD 347–407)—Raised and educated in Syrian Antioch, Chrysostom served as the bishop of Constantinople (modern Istanbul) from 398 until his death. A prolific author, he received his title *chrysostomos* (Greek for "goldenmouthed") out of respect for his reputation as a renowned preacher. He was constantly opposed in church politics by Theophilus, bishop of Alexandria, and eventually was exiled to a village on the Black Sea.

Justin Martyr (died ca. AD 165)—Born and raised in Syrian Palestine, Justin was a second-century author, teacher, and interpreter of scripture. He was a vigorous champion of early Christian traditions against the threats of pagan philosophies, Rome, Judaism, and various heresies. After an extended and active ministry, Justin was eventually tortured and beheaded under the Roman prefect Junius Rusticus (162–168).

Manual of Discipline—Also known as the Community Rule, this text is one of the oldest documents from the ancient community of Qumran, a Jewish sect which flourished on the western banks of the Dead Sea from roughly the second century BC to the second century AD. Written for the leaders of the community, the text includes instructions on correct liturgy, rites of initiation into the sect, rules for the common life, and issues of communal organization and discipline.

Marcion (died ca. AD 154)—Born in Sinope of Asia Minor, Marcion became a member of the church in Rome around the year 140 but was expelled four years later for his gnostic beliefs. Soon he began his own organized church, and his ideas became widely disseminated. A devoted advocate of the apostle Paul's teaching, Marcion created the first known New Testament canon, which included the Gospel of Luke and ten letters attributed to Paul.

Marcus Aurelius (AD 121–180)—Emperor of Rome (161–180) and a noted Stoic philosopher, Aurelius considered Christianity to be a threat to the official religion of the Roman Empire—emperor worship. During his years of rule, he allowed the widespread persecution of Christians in his attempt to protect the place of Greek philosophy.

Melito of Sardis (late second century AD)—Bishop at the end of the second century AD, Melito is known primarily from the witness of Eusebius of Caesarea. Though he authored several writings, his fragmentary homily *On the Passover* is all that remains. Melito's vivid rhetorical style, anti-Jewish bias, and high Christology have received significant scholarly attention.

midrash—An approach to scripture which means "interpretation." Midrash was the primary tool of those numerous Jewish scholars associated with the rise of rabbinic literature. Midrash gives careful attention to the meaning of individual words and phrases, and freely interprets any textual passage against another, regardless of context. This method assumes that there are countless meanings behind scripture that may be discerned through the appropriate study of the materials.

Montanism—An early Christian prophetic movement prevalent in Asia Minor during the late second through fourth centuries AD. The movement was named after the ecstatic prophet Montanus (ca. 170), who insisted that a true prophet could not be restricted by the rational mind. He eventually was excommunicated by Eleutherus, bishop of Rome, in the year 177. The most famous follower of the movement was the third-century apologist Tertullian of Carthage.

Muratorian canon—An ancient Christian Latin codex containing texts from the early church. There is some debate as to whether this canon of writings was produced at the end of the second century or, instead, later in the fourth century. In either case, the value of the text lies in its attestation to those gospels and letters that were most widely used by early Christians.

mystery religions—Several religions of the ancient Greek, Persian, and Egyptian worlds are classified today as *mystery religions*. Though little is known about them, since their rituals and beliefs were held in secret by their members, their influence permeated much of early Christian thought and is thought by many theologians to have threatened the theological development of the early church.

Nerva (AD 35–98)—Grandson of the emperor Tiberius, Nerva became emperor in 96 after the death of Domitian. He ruled for only sixteen months. He was more tolerant of Christianity and Judaism than was his predecessor, though his influence on the Roman Empire was brief and ephemeral. Eusebius of Caesarea reports that during Nerva's reign the apostle John was permitted to return from exile and resume residence in the city of Ephesus.

Nero (AD 37–68)—The last Roman emperor in the line of Augustus Caesar, Nero reigned during the years 54–68. Being suspicious of friends and enemies alike, Nero conducted a reign of terror against his opponents during the last years of his rule. After he blamed the Christians of Rome for the fire which engulfed the city in 64, Nero executed numerous individuals as scapegoats for his own political problems.

numerology—The belief that special insights may be derived from the study of number patterns and the combination of numbers. This common idea throughout the ancient world arises in Christian literature as a tool for use in the interpretation of historical events and texts. Certain numbers are special within the Jewish-Christian tradition (for example—3, 4, 7, 12, 40), as well as the appearance of such numbers in statistical combinations (for example—144 = 12 x 12).

Origen (ca. AD 185–ca. 251)—The premier theologian of the so-called Alexandrian school of Christian instruction, Origen appears to have been a student of Clement of Alexandria. He traveled extensively throughout the Roman Empire and soon developed a reputation as a prolific author. Among Origen's more prominent writings are the work *Against Celsus*, which is a defense of Christianity, and his tractate *On First Principles*, an investigation into the foundations of faith and theology.

Pantaenus of Alexandria (late second century AD)—A Christian scholar who pursued the spiritual interpretation of scripture. Originally from Sicily, Pantaenus is perhaps best known as the founder of the famous catechetical school at Alexandria. He attempted to link Christian principles with Greek philosophy, a task which continued to develop in the work of his most famous pupil—Clement of Alexandria.

patristics—The field of historical research which is concerned for the writings of early Christianity. Each text is considered to be authored by a "father" (in Latin, *pater*) of the tradition. There are no specific dates which define the limits of this study, though most patristic scholars work with Christian literature which was written during the first six centuries AD.

Philo of Alexandria (ca. 20 BC–ca. AD 50)—The son of a prominent Jewish family in Alexandria, Philo wrote extensively about Jewish theology and Greek philosophy. He was convinced that Judaism and Greek culture could be successfully welded into a coherent view of the world, a view which was endorsed by the hidden meanings of the Hebrew Scriptures. Philo's writings became a source of inspiration and study in early Christian Egypt.

Pionius (died AD 250)—A third-century presbyter of Smyrna in Asia Minor who was martyred during the persecutions of the emperor Decius. A prominent speaker whose travels were extensive, Pionius has been falsely credited with writing the fifth-century tractate *A Life of Polycarp*.

Pius I (bishop ca. AD 140–154)—Though a bishop in the city of Rome at the middle of the second century, little specific information is known about Pius (Pope Pius I). The influence of the church in Rome spread throughout the Roman Empire during his leadership, as did gnosticism. He is known to have been visited by such notable Christians as Polycarp of Smyrna, Justin Martyr, and Irenaeus of Lyons.

pseudepigraph—This term, which literally means "false writing," refers to ancient texts that were composed by one author yet attributed to another person. The practice was considered to be a legitimate way in which to honor a renowned person, to offer further comments which were in harmony with an ancient author or theologian, or to gain acceptance or authority for a particular text.

Pseudo-Clementines—A collection of early Christian writings that became associated with the name of Clement of Rome (first century AD). These texts, which originated in fourth-century Syria, now appear in two primary sections—the *Homilies* and the *Recognitions*—though they initially formed a single writing. Preserved here is a clear witness to an early form of Jewish Christianity which eventually disappeared during the formation of the orthodox church tradition.

Septuagint—Often cited as "LXX" (for the seventy[-two] translators), this was the early Greek translation of the Old Testament or Hebrew Scriptures. The Septuagint has been dated to the third through second centuries BC and was produced in Alexandria, Egypt. This version of the scriptures was used by Jews and Christians alike and became a ready source for the development of early Christian theology.

Serapion of Thmuis (died after AD 362)—A fourth-century monk, Serapion became bishop of the city of Thmuis in the Nile Delta during the year 339. He wrote some thirty letters and a treatise against the heresy of Manichaeism. Records indicate that he was a close friend of the famous monk Antony in Egypt and the bishop Athanasius of Alexandria.

Soter (died ca. AD 174)—Bishop of Rome during the years AD 166–174, Soter guided the Roman church during the reign of the emperor Marcus Aurelius (161–180). Little information remains about his tenure as bishop. Soter is known to have communicated with the church at Corinth, however, and to have established the timing of Easter as a yearly festival in the church of Rome.

stoicism—Founded by the Greek philosopher Zeno (ca. 333–262 BC), this world view became a popular philosophy within Greek and Roman culture. Stoic philosophy insisted that the divine principle of life—*logos* or reason—gave order to the world and could be found in all creatures and substances. Though generally rejected by early Christian authors, Stoic thought was popular among the Christian theologians of Alexandria in Egypt.

synoptic gospels—Scholars often refer to the first three gospels of the New Testament canon—Matthew, Mark, Luke—as the synoptic gospels, which comes from the Greek expression *to see together* or *to see all at once*. This term is meant to indicate that these gospels in many ways share a common understanding about the life and works of Jesus of Nazareth that is distinct from the view which is offered by the Gospel of John.

Tatian (second century AD)—An early Christian apologist, Tatian was a student of Justin Martyr. Born in eastern Syria, he founded a catechetical school in Mesopotamia and wrote extensively in defense of the early Christian faith. Tatian's most famous writing, the *Diatessaron*, was a harmony of the New Testament gospels and was widely used in Syrian communities until the fifth century.

testimonia—This term refers to collections of early church proof texts assembled from the literature of the Old Testament. These often were drawn from a single writing and were linked together according to theme. Such collections allowed the transmission of essential doctrines, beliefs, and principles of Christian theology and formed a limited corpus of authoritative teachings for composing homilies.

Theophilus of Antioch (late second century AD)—An adult convert to Christianity, Theophilus was an early Christian apologist and bishop. He was well educated in Greek philosophy and attacked the views of pagan idol worship. A prolific author, most of his writings are now lost.

Trajan (AD 53–117)—Born in Spain, Trajan became emperor of Rome at the death of Nerva in 98. It was during his reign that the legal status of Christianity perhaps was debated the most vigorously. This is reflected in the 121 letters between the emperor and Pliny, governor of Pontus-Bithynia. Ancient historians considered Trajan to be an ideal emperor.

transubstantiation—The Roman Catholic dogma or belief that the substance of the bread and wine at the celebration of the eucharist is transformed into the body and blood of Christ. This transformation is achieved through the power of God as a mystery of the church. Other Christian traditions typically view these elements of the meal as symbols of the death and resurrection of Jesus of Nazareth, or as seals of the unity of the community of believers.

Vulgate—Jerome's Latin translation of the scriptures at the beginning of the fifth century AD. Jerome produced the Vulgate in order to revise the many older Latin texts circulating in Western Christendom. His translation, which became the primary text of the church throughout the Medieval period, eventually assumed many forms according to the numerous scribes who copied the text.

Index of
Ancient Literature